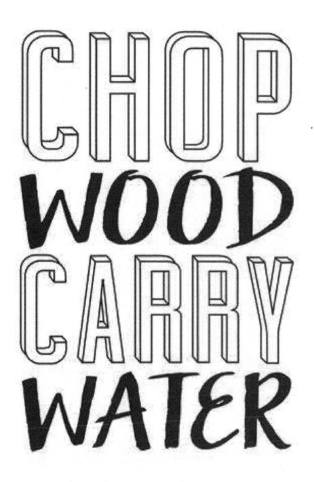

CHOP WOOD CARRY WATER

HOW TO FALL IN LOVE WITH THE PROCESS OF BECOMING GREAT

Joshua Medcalf

Table of Contents

Chop Wood, Carry Water

For as long as his family could remember, John and his younger brother Jordan had been in love with the samurai culture of Japan. When John was only eight years old, his family visited many places in Asia. He and Jordan excitedly explored every place they visited, and dreamt of returning one day to become their favorite type of samurai warriors: <u>archers</u>.

A year later, tragedy struck as the family was in a bad car accident and Jordan was severely injured. The rest of the family was pretty banged up, but Jordan was barely hanging onto life in the ICU. For the first few months John sat at his bedside, only leaving the hospital to shower two times a week, reading him stories throughout the day of the samurai culture that they both loved so much. Every night they would fall asleep to Jackie Chan movies. John's parents even let him miss the first month of school.

Eventually after five months of being in the hospital Jordan was cleared to go home. The doctors said he would never again be able to talk, walk, or feed himself. Jordan still found ways to communicate and play with John and they became even more close than they were before the accident. John always admired his brothers positive attitude despite his circumstances. The doctors said for Jordan to go through a normal day it required as much energy as it does for an average person to run a marathon.

As John entered his teenage years, he never forgot their shared love of the samurai, and over time his fascination turned to deep admiration and lasting respect. He began to think more and more about pursuing it in his future.

Finally, when he turned eighteen, John bought a one-way ticket to an ancient city in Japan, intent on fulfilling his boyhood dream. He enrolled as an apprentice to a small community of samurai who lived outside the city walls, practicing their timeless traditions. There, he knew he could become a samurai archer.

When John arrived, he was greeted by a friendly old sensei named Akira. He helped John unload his bags and get settled. As they walked the grounds, taking a look at the advanced training areas and shooting ranges, John grew more and more excited. This place was amazing! He couldn't wait to get started.

But the next morning, Akira gathered the newly-arrived apprentices and informed them of their first task: for the rest of the morning, they must chop wood and carry water.

John was surprised and confused. He addressed his teacher with the proper title of respect that they had been taught: "Akira-sensei, what do you mean?"

The old man explained that their community was outfitted with every modern convenience, except for heat and running water. Instead of using gas or electricity, they burned wood for heat when the weather grew cold. And in order to use water in the bathrooms and kitchen, it must be brought by hand from a well outside. Thus, in order for the community to use water and stay warm during the winter, the community depended on everyone to chop wood and carry water.

"But when will we get to shoot?" John wondered aloud.

Akira just smiled. "Shooting will come soon enough. But first you must chop wood, and carry water."

John was frustrated, but he obeyed. He trusted his sensei's wisdom, and knew that in time, they would move on to more exciting things.

Building Your Own House

The next day was hot and muggy. John sweated as he drove his axe through log after log. His shoulders ached as he hauled bucket after bucket of water from the well into the house, and his hands began to blister from the friction of the axe handle. It was frustrating watching men old enough to be in retirement homes chop wood and carry water so effortlessly. But he kept working, remembering Akira's words that, "shooting will come soon enough."

Finally, after the day's work had finished, Akira took John aside. He handed him a cup of cool water and told him a story.

He told John that in Japan they have a deep love of architecture, and there once was a man named Kota who built some of the finest houses in all of Tokyo. His work became world famous due to his dedication to the process, his willingness to beat on his craft, and his relentless devotion to keep learning, even late into his career.

Eventually though, Kota grew tired of building homes for other people and he was ready to retire. He had been building homes for over thirty years, and he was ready to move on. He wanted to travel and spend lots of time with his grandkids.

One day, Kota approached his boss, and turned in his two week notice.

His boss said, "Kota, we are forever indebted to you for the magnificent work you have done for our company, and we are so grateful you have worked for us for so long. We do have one favor to ask of you though. Could you please build one more house? It is a very important house, for a very important client, and everyone in the company agreed it needs your special touch!"

Kota was frustrated. He would have to cancel two trips and postpone his new life, all for one house. He told his boss that he needed a day to think about it. After talking it over with his wife, he gave in and decided he would build one more house. But he told his boss, "This is the very last one!"

But while Kota had agreed with his *head* to build this last house, his *heart* was no longer in it. He had always been very hands-on through the entire building process, always selecting the finest materials by hand and making sure every detail was diligently tended to.

But this house was different.

He viewed it more as an *obligation* than an *opportunity*. He delegated much of the work, and consequently a lot of things started slipping through the cracks. The house would be up to code, but as it started to come together, it was obvious that it lacked the "wow" factor that Kota's other homes were known for.

Kota knew in his heart that this was far from his best work, but he was over it and ready to move on to the next phase of his life. The *next* phase was much more appealing and important to him than the *present* moment.

After four months had passed, Kota finally finished the house.

He went back to his boss, telling him, "I did what you asked. Now I am asking, one last time, for your blessing to retire."

His boss said, "Thank you Kota! We just have one more thing!"

Now Kota was beginning to get really upset because he thought they were going to ask him to build another house.

His boss reached into his desk and pulled out a very small black box with a red ribbon tied around it. He handed the box to Kota, and said, "We are so grateful for you, Kota. This gift is a token of our appreciation."

Kota pulled the ribbon, opening the box to discover a set of shiny new keys. His boss smiled, "The house is yours! You deserve it!"

Immediately, his heart sank. Unbeknownst to Kota, *the whole time he had been building his own house.* If he had only known the house was his own, he would have cared so much more. He would have only used the finest materials, and he would have overseen every detail and given it his all like he had always done. But now, it was too late.

Akira looked at John and said, "The only thing that is truly significant about today, or any other day, is who you become in the process. Think about it, John. What good is it to reach the top if you skip steps to get there? Would you want the person flying your plane, performing your surgery, or handling your money to have cheated?

Each of us are building our own house. Sometimes you might think you are building for your school, your family, your company, or your team, but you are always building your own house... *I hope you build wisely.*"

The story hit home for John and he really started to think deeply about his own life. He sat in silent contemplation while wondering if he had been building his house wisely.

3

How much is an inch worth?

The next day, the sun rose, and so did John, with a burst of energy. He couldn't wait to get started on his "real" training. He rushed through the hours of chopping wood and carrying water, then raced to the archery range, excited to begin.

But instead, Akira announced that they would focus simply on the basics of their stance and drawing motion, without nocking a single arrow.

John couldn't keep the disappointment from his voice, "Akira-sensei, I thought you said we'd be shooting soon?"

The old man shook his head. "I said that shooting would come soon enough. First, you must learn how to stand."

John swallowed his pride and obeyed, lining up with the other apprentices. Still, he couldn't help but think, "*'Learn' how to stand? I know how to stand! What could I possibly not know about standing?*" As it turned out, quite a bit. Akira gently and persistently adjusted John's every tiny motion, using a thin bamboo rod to nudge an elbow or prod a knee into place. Yet none of the adjustments were more than an inch, which surprised John greatly.

"Are you sure this matters? It's just an inch."

"Ah, but it is so much more than that." Akira handed John an arrow. "Draw and release."

John obeyed, sending the arrow sailing — THWACKK! Into the straw target.

"Now, draw again and hold."

John obeyed, locking his form at full draw. Using the rod, Akira subtly adjusted John's elbow, less than even an inch, and stepped back.

"Release."

John obeyed, but — WHOOSH! The arrow sailed wide, barely grazing the target as it disappeared into the forest beyond. John couldn't believe his eyes.

Akira smiled. "Now you see how much an inch is worth. Every adjustment at the firing line means the difference between hitting the target or missing it. And the same is true in life. Every little thing we do, no matter how mundane, matters greatly when it is multiplied by the number of times we do it. Over time, even the smallest habit or choice can change our lives immensely. Do you know what separates most wildly successful people from everyone else, John?"

"Luck?" Akira shook his head, *no*. "Hard work?" Again, *no*. "Coming from the right background?"

Akira just smiled, "Inches, John. That's all that separates them."

John nodded, but still had trouble grasping it. *Could that really be true?* Sensing his hesitation, Akira continued...

"Think about your group of friends from high school. You're all from the same area, you're all the same age, and most of you have had a very similar set of opportunities. And right now, someone might look at all of you and be unable to really see much of a difference. But in ten years? The differences in your lives will be night and day. Someone you might have thought of as an underachiever might be incredibly successful, while another who flourished in high school may be struggling to even survive. But I can assure you, the difference in their lives will always come down to inches.

Most people are so consumed with their day-to-day lives, that they never pause to see the big picture. And in the big picture, every single choice matters, no matter how small. Everything you choose to read, listen to, or look at. Everything you think about, dream about, or focus on. And especially, your circle — the people you surround yourself with and allow to influence you — can make all the difference in who you become. Inches might look small up close, but added up over the right amount of time, they can cover any distance in the universe."

John nodded, beginning to understand. "I guess I never thought of that."

"The most amazing thing is, John, that all of those choices are very easy to make. It's not difficult to read ten pages of a great book each day, or take a walk for twenty minutes each day to stay healthy, or to call your parents or a friend every week to maintain a relationship. But it's also just as easy not to do those things. For example, think about eating: every day around the world, millions of people choose to consume fatty, sugary foods that, over time, will clog their arteries and kill them. This is no secret to anyone, and yet it happens every day. Why is that?"

John shrugged, blank, as Akira continued: "Because those foods won't kill them today. Today, it's just a hamburger, or a hot dog, or a soda. It doesn't seem like much. And of course, eating something like that once in a while isn't terrible. But in the long run, if you choose to eat it every day? That choice, <u>that inch</u>, can be the difference between life and death.

You will make many choices during your time here training, John. They might not look like much at first, but I promise you that over the next ten years, they will add up, and make all the difference in whether or not you fulfill your true potential and live your dreams."

"I'll share with you one of the greatest pieces of wisdom for your journey, *"Greatness isn't for the chosen few. Greatness is for the few who choose."*[1]

---

1 Quote from Jamie Gilbert

4

Artificial Maturity

As the weeks passed, John grew more comfortable with life in the community. As his form straightened and improved, he was allowed to begin working with arrows, even though he and the other apprentices were limited to shooting only at practice targets, straw rolls only seven feet away.

But still, he persisted, trying to focus on everything each sensei taught him.

One day, as he drew his bow, ready to release the arrow — SNAPP!! The bowstring split, leaving John with an unstrung bow. He quickly unpacked a new one from the apprentices' bowstring roll.

Akira approached, watching with interest as John unraveled the new bowstring, trying to make sense of it. He slowly raised an eyebrow. "John, have you done this before?"

John shook his head, but he wasn't worried. "Not personally. But I've seen it done."

"So, you know how to re-string it?"

John beamed with confidence. "Of course! I've read about it dozens of times, and like I said, I've seen it too. I watched a lot of videos on YouTube."

Calmly, Akira nodded. "Good. Then I won't stop you."

Concentrating hard, John slipped the top loop of the new bowstring snugly over the top end of his bow. Then, he knelt, gently bending the bow toward him as he guided the bottom loop toward the bow's bottom end. But as he tried to slip the knotted bowstring over the notch, he couldn't quite get it to fit correctly. It kept sliding all over the place, made even more difficult by the slick resin coating the brand-new bowstring.

John tried a few more times, getting more and more frustrated each time. Akira just watched in silence, until finally John exclaimed in pure frustration, "What the heck is wrong with this thing? Why can't I get it to work?"

Akira replied calmly, "Because, John. You only have *ginōsko* of it."

John thought he'd just heard wrong. "What?!"

Akira grinned, "If that sounded like Greek to you, that's because it is. '*Ginōsko*' is a Greek word that means to have knowledge <u>of</u> something, as opposed to '*yāda*,' which means knowledge gained <u>through experiencing</u> something. The two are very different."

John nodded to his still-un-strung bow. "I'll say they are!"

"Who would you want to go into battle with John? Someone who has studied and read about war for 25 years, or someone who has trained and experienced the front lines of battle?"

"Well, when you put it that way, I want the person who has the real experience in battle." Said John.

"A ancient warrior once said, "It is one thing to study war and another to live the warrior's life."[2] In a world where anyone can look up information online, it's deceptively easy to gain "knowledge." You can get pretty confident by reading everything you can get your hands on about a certain subject, it's called "artificial maturity."[3] But knowing about how to do something and having practical experience actually doing something are radically different."

John sighed, "I guess I've got a long way to go."

Akira smiled, handing John a pouch of fine, granulated powder.

"You might want to start with this. The powder gives the bowstring some grip, and stops it from slipping off the wood."

Excited, John coated the string with the powder, and as Akira guided him, finally slipped it over the wood, re-stringing the bow. With a grin, he leapt back to the firing line and began to practice again, thankful for such a kind and patient mentor.

---

2   Telamon of Arcadia from *The War of Art*
3   Concept coined by Tim Elmore

5

Faithful in the Small Things

As the weeks passed, John grew more comfortable with life in the community. One day, he woke up to find all the other apprentices crowding excitedly around an announcement that had been posted in the dining hall. It announced that each year, the incoming class of apprentices would be able to compete in an archery tournament.

John could barely contain his excitement. He loved competition, and he was intent on winning the tournament.

He couldn't stop talking about it that morning as he finished his daily routine. Finally, Akira grabbed his shoulders, and sat him down. He looked deep into John's eyes.

"John, Mother Theresa always told people, 'Be faithful in the small things, for it is in them that your strength lies.' The temptation while you are here with us will to be to focus on all the big sexy goals, like winning the tournament, and becoming a great samurai archer. You must fight that temptation, and stay focused on chopping wood and carrying water. Do you recognize the name *Ingvar Kamprad?*"

John shook his head, no.

"Good!" Akira smiled wide. "Ingvar was a young boy who spent four or five years selling individual matchsticks door to door in his small town in Sweden. He was often laughed at when he would tell the other boys he couldn't play, because he needed to ride his bike three hours into Stockholm to purchase another box of matches."

John couldn't believe his ears. "Hold on! You mean to tell me that this little kid was really selling individual matchsticks door to door, for years?!"

"Yes, John. This is a true story. When Ingvar was seventeen years old he decided to name his company. You might have heard of it: *Ikea* is worth over one hundred fifty billion dollars today."

John listened in awe as Akira continued.

"John, everyone wants to start the next Ikea, but few are willing to be faithful selling individual matchsticks door to door. Everyone wants to build the next Apple or Facebook, *nobody* wants to sell matches. Everyone wants to become a samurai warrior, but few are willing to faithfully chop wood, carry water.

Every now and then a person comes along and accidentally gets it the first time, but most of us have to learn the hard way through multiple failed experiments, which allows us to learn lessons and skills those who had it easier did not develop.

Steve Jobs didn't set out to transform entertainment, computers, music, tele-communications, and education. It happened as a byproduct of passion, persistence, and faithfulness to a small idea.

The problem with small is that it isn't sexy, and it's often boring.

A guy who played professional golf, was once hit by a bus and the people serving as his doctors told him he would never walk again. But he trained hard, day in and day out, and went on to win a *major*. He said, 'Everyone thinks greatness is sexy, it's not. It's dirty, hard work.'

Ingvar didn't have a sexy idea, he had an idea most people would laugh at today. I can't even imagine how much grief he took from friends and family. 'You are doing <u>what</u>?! That is the stupidest idea ever!'

Everyone wants to win championships, but nobody wants to sweep the barn they practice in like John Wooden did for his first few years in Westwood.

Everyone wants to be great, until it's time to do what greatness requires.

Don't believe the myths. Greatness is far from sexy, it is dirty, hard work, usually required to be done in the dark, when no one is watching, while your dreams are so far off they feel like fairytales.

> Dream BIG.
> Start small.
> Be ridiculously faithful.
> Focus on what you can control.

Your greatest challenge during your time here will be faithfully keeping your focus on the process, while surrendering the outcome."

John nodded his head in acknowledgement, but the truth was more than he could handle. He thought he understood, but some things can only be experienced to be fully learned.

6

One Eye For the Journey

After the excitement of the first few months had started to wear off, John began to get frustrated. The monotony of chopping wood and carrying water every morning and every evening had begun to wear on him.

He was only allowed to practice archery for four hours, during the heat of the day. What frustrated him the most, was that he was only allowed to shoot at a straw roll that was only seven feet away from him. He and the other apprentices were also required to attend weekly workshops where they learned life skills and lessons through stories.

One day he approached Akira and asked, "Akira-sensei, how long will it take me to become a samurai archer? I have dreamed my whole life of being one, but it feels like it will take forever."

Akira stopped what he was doing and said, "In the West, you want everything instantly, but here you must learn to fall in love with the process of becoming great. Now go chop wood, and carry water."

John was confused, but he went back to his normal daily activities.

The months passed, and before he knew it, an entire year had gone by. During the first year 'acclimation period' apprentices are not allowed to speak with their family and friends. When John was finally able to have a Skype video call with his family, he was disappointed to share with them that he hadn't moved past shooting at a target only seven feet away from him, and that the rest of his time each day was spent chopping wood and carrying water.

As John talked about his daily routine, his father got a big smile on his face. He asked John who his favorite basketball players were growing up. John replied, "That's easy: Kobe Bryant and Michael Jordan."

His dad then told him how Phil Jackson had just released a book, *Eleven Rings*, and how he was constantly telling the guys on his teams about the necessity of "chop wood, carry water." No matter whether you are winning or losing, the point was to focus on the *process* and neither get too high or too low, but instead to control the controllables.

After the call, John's spirits were much better. It was especially hard being away from Jordan, and just seeing him was encouraging to John.

A few months went by, and as John practiced, his muscles began to learn the familiar motions of drawing and releasing, and his shots grew more accurate. He began to feel very confident with his bow and hitting the seven-foot target.

One day while he was practicing, Akira walked over and John asked again, "Akira-sensei, I am getting better and better each week. How long will it take for me to become a samurai archer now?"

Akira smiled, and told him it would take ten years.

John was furious. "Ten years? Maybe if I didn't have to spend so much time chopping wood and carrying water then I would be able to reach my goal much faster!"

Akira replied, "If you don't chop wood and carry water, then it will take you twenty years to become a samurai archer." Then he turned and walked away.

John was even more confused, and he questioned whether or not he should quit. Would it really take him ten years? He wasn't sure this investment was worth it, but decided he would try even harder.

More time passed, and John's shots became more accurate and more powerful. He came to love the sound of the arrow slamming into the target. THWACK!! THWACK!!

Soon, he was certain that he could become a samurai archer in less than ten years.

So one day, as they were carrying water back from the well, he pulled Akira aside and asked, "Akira-sensei, I am more accurate now and my shots are more powerful than ever. How long will it take me to become a samurai archer?"

Akira smiled. "You know the answer. It is still ten years."

John kept pressing, "But what if I devote every waking moment to becoming a samurai archer? No chopping wood or carrying water, just archery."

But Akira only shrugged. "Then, it will take thirty years."

John had reached his emotional breaking point. He blurted out, "But I don't understand!"

Akira looked at John with compassion. "You will learn, young John, the reason it takes longer is because with one eye on the goal, you only have one eye for the journey."

He then went on to tell John stories of people who climb ice mountains, and how if they are focused on the top of the mountain they will not know where to step in front of them. They will slip and die. The key to ice climbing is to focus on one solid step at a time. "No man climbs a mountain all at once. He climbs it by making one solid step at a time."

John nodded, he understood now. He would try to focus on doing his best at archery, chopping wood, carrying water, and letting go of the result.

Nothing is a Test

But try as he might, John kept unconsciously slipping back into his old habits. Growing up, he had always succeeded in sports and school by focusing on proving himself. Some of his coaches even told him they liked the way he played with a chip on his shoulder, and even in the peaceful environment of the samurai community it was hard for him to shake those instincts of seeing life as one test after another to prove his worth.

Without realizing it, he began to pride himself on completing each drill and archery movement the fastest, and even made sure that he chopped more wood and carried more water in less time than the other apprentices.

One day, he was so focused on this that he filled his buckets well above the normal level. Walking briskly toward the community house, his foot caught the lip of an old root buried in the ground, and the weight of the water in his buckets sent him toppling over! He slammed to the ground, soaked to the bone.

But just as he opened his mouth to shout in anger, he noticed Akira watching him. The old sensei had seen the whole thing, and as John picked himself painfully up off the ground, Akira pulled John to his feet, picked up one of his buckets, and walked with him back toward the well.

"You were carrying quite a lot of water, weren't you?" he asked.

John shrugged, trying to play it off. "I guess. I don't think about it. I just try to carry the most that I can."

Akira saw through this, asking quietly, "The most that you can, or just *more* than any of the others?"

John reddened, caught, as Akira went on. "John, you keep getting in the way of your own potential, because you keep seeing everything as a test. The secret is to understand that nothing is a test, but only an opportunity to learn and grow. Many people never fulfill their potential, because they look at every situation in life as a test.

If you look at something as a test, then you will focus only on passing the test instead of maximizing your growth through the experience. Over time, the person who is simply focused on maximizing what they can learn and how they can grow will become much greater than the person who sees life as one continual test to prove themselves."

John nodded, struggling with that wisdom.

"Don't fall for the trap, John. Even tests in school are not tests. Nothing is a test, it's only an illusion. Everything is an opportunity to learn and grow, because remember, you are building your own house."

Where Do You Find Your Identity?

As time passed, despite Akira's warnings, John grew more and more intently focused on his goal of becoming a samurai archer. He even began to sneak in extra time at the range. Every night at dusk, he would slip away from the dining hall and down to the range, where he'd shoot until darkness fell.

But over time, the extra practice began to wear on his body. Then, one afternoon at the range, he began to feel a burning tightness as he drew his bow, which became increasingly painful as he locked his shoulder into the firing position. He pushed through it, forcing his body to repeat the motion, but soon the pain in his shoulder made firing his bow impossible. He cringed, as...

"What's wrong, John?"

Akira walked toward him, concerned. Clearly, the old sensei had noticed the pain in John's eyes. John knew there was no way to hide it.

The next thing he knew, he was in the infirmary, getting his shoulder wrapped. Akira explained his injury, telling him, "Practice is good, but too much practice is not. Your muscles have torn, and they need time and rest in order to heal."

"How long?"

"Six to eight weeks."

John's face fell, as he realized that because of this, he would fall far behind in his program.

Seeing this, Akira asked him a question: "John, who would you *be* if everything you *do* was taken away from you?"

"What do you mean, Akira-sensei?"

"I mean that right now, you are not an archer. You can't even shoot. So, who are you?"

John thought for a minute, becoming frustrated as he realized: *he didn't have a good answer.*

Akira nodded, understanding. "Do not worry. Even I fall into this trap, John. It is so easy for me to get caught up in the results I get from working with people, to get lost in the work or in the response from my archers. I constantly have to remind myself that my value comes from who I am, *not* from what I do.

It is easy to feel like your value is much greater when your teams win, when you make a lot of money, when you experience great success in business. But it is just as easy to feel defeated and depressed when your teams aren't winning, when your business is failing, and when it feels like you are failing at *everything*.

The truth is that your value is constant, it is priceless, and it never truly goes up or down based off of results or your performance. *Your value comes from who you are, not from what you do. Every human being is infinitely priceless.*

You are more than an athlete.
You are more than a parent, a brother, a daughter.
You are more than a coach.
You are more than a CEO.
You are more than a fast food worker.

When your identity gets wrapped up in what you do, it clouds every decision you make. It is easy to see some of the reasons that a person would make very compromising decisions when their identity comes from what they do. You must fight that instinct."

John nodded, realizing the truth in his sensei's words.

Akira stood to go, leaving John with this: "Here is my challenge for you during your time here, John. Find your identity in something that cannot simply be stripped away in a moment, but instead do the hard work of reminding yourself that your value comes from who you are. For me, and it took me a long time to grasp this, but my identity comes from being a child of God, and that He recklessly and unconditionally loves me.

I believe He feels the same way about you, and already unconditionally loves you. It has never been about your performance, and it never will be about your performance. You can't do anything to make Him love you any more, and you can't do anything to make Him love you any less. Therefore, you are free to accept His love, love Him back, love yourself, and finally be freed to love others with no strings attached.

I do not expect you to believe everything that I believe John. You must come to your own conclusions. Whatever you do though, please don't find your identity in something that can be gone in a moment's notice."

9

Uncomfortable isn't a Choice

One of the hardest things for John to grow accustomed to in his new life was the fact that he must train every day, no matter how cold or wet. The only thing that stopped their training was lightning. He had grown up amidst sunshine and warmth, so adjusting to the biting chill of a winter wind or the gusting rain of the summer monsoon season was difficult for him.

One day in particular, as the bright colors of autumn began to fade from the trees, an ice-cold wind swept through, so piercing that it seemed to go right through his clothes and into his bones. As John shot arrow after arrow, he couldn't stop shivering. In fact, he was shivering so badly that it began to affect his aim. He struggled again and again, but couldn't seem to find a rhythm in his shots.

Akira noticed, walking over. "What's going on, John? I couldn't help but notice you seem to be having some trouble."

John nodded, fighting to keep his teeth from chattering. "I feel like I'm going to freeze to death!"

But instead of acknowledging the cold, Akira simply replied: "Let me ask you a question. Where would you rather be uncomfortable: here in training, or under the bright lights?"

John thought hard about it. "Here, I guess."

"That's right. *Uncomfortable isn't a choice, but where you experience it is.* Life will always be difficult somewhere. But we can choose to experience that difficulty now, or push it off until later. Everything costs something. Nothing comes free. Hard isn't a choice, but where you experience it is.

Some people say, "it's too hard." Guess what, so is being broke. So is failing to come close to your potential. So is the pain of regret." Akira just shook his head, obviously frustrated with people who had failed to heed his warnings in the past.

"Do you know who the Navy SEALs are, John?"

John's eyes lit up at the mention of the most elite group of warriors in the modern world: "Of course! They're the toughest soldiers on the planet!"

"Do you know why? Because their training is the toughest on the planet. Week after week of non-stop misery. No sleep, extreme weather, and drill after drill where they're pushed past every single human limit, both mentally and physically. Eighty percent of the men who enter SEAL training drop out, many because their bodies simply shut down. I met a SEAL once, and I asked him why they put themselves through such extreme circumstances. And I'll never forget what he told me...

'*Under pressure you don't rise to the occasion, you sink to the level of your training. That is why we train so hard.*'

John, I wouldn't be a very good sensei if I did you the disservice of putting you through comfortable training every day. Because later on, under pressure, you would crumble.

I always get angry when I hear someone say, 'It's too hard!' when they're faced with the choice to do something difficult in the moment that will pay off in the long run. Because I can guarantee you that no matter how hard it might be, the pain of regret after <u>not</u> doing it is much harder. Being broke is a lot harder than saving a percentage of every paycheck. Living with diabetes is a lot harder than limiting how much sugar you consume each day. And failing to come close to your God-given potential and ending up in a dead-end job that's robbing you of your time and slowly killing your heart is *much* harder than betting on yourself and taking the scary leap into what you know you should do with your life.

You don't find any traffic after going the extra mile, and there's a very good reason for that: most people won't do what it takes to get there. But if you choose to do what others won't, eventually you will get to do what others can't.

Let me tell you a secret. People who get average results persist until things get uncomfortable, then they quit. People who get good results persist until things get painful, then they quit. People who get world class results have trained themselves to become comfortable when it is painful and uncomfortable.

You can't cheat the grind, John. It knows how hard you have worked, and it won't give you anything you have not earned.

John, do you know why they say "the ball doesn't lie"? Because you can't cheat the person in the mirror. Deep down *you know* whether you have cut corners and cheated, and subconsciously that is incredible hard to overcome.

This is why we shoot every day, no matter the weather. So that when the pressure comes and you sink to the level of your training, you really aren't sinking at all, but are instead pushed up and supported by all those hours you've spent training hard."

John nodded, energized. "Thank you, Akira-sensei. I'll work on learning to embrace what's uncomfortable now, knowing all the while that it's keeping me from the much bigger pain of regret later on!"

10

Guzzling Salt Water

Once a week, the apprentices were allowed to watch television. John and Akira started to form a bond watching American sports together. One of their favorite teams to watch was the Los Angeles Lakers. One night, Akira began to speak to the apprentices about the importance of creating a new scorecard for life.

He pointed to Kobe Bryant as Kobe drained another three-pointer. "Tell me, why is Kobe Bryant still playing basketball?"

The apprentices watched Kobe hustle. John answered, "Because he loves basketball?"

"Yes, possibly, but he has repeatedly said that if he wins his <u>sixth</u> NBA title, *then* he will be satisfied and retire. Kobe isn't the only one who has fallen for this trap. Every day, people everywhere live their lives believing that everything will be different if they can just achieve more, win more, or make more money. But if achievement hasn't filled that void to date, how is achieving *more* going to fill it in the future?

Like thirsty people guzzling salt water, achievement only creates a greater desire for accomplishing more, dehydrating us of true satisfaction and fulfillment.

After Andre Agassi made it to number one in the world in tennis, he said, 'I thought that getting to number one was going to be the moment

I made sense of my life. But it left me a little empty, and I spiraled down.'

Have you ever noticed that some of the most outwardly beautiful people on earth seemingly have the most troubling relationships, or that some of the wealthiest people have the most sleepless nights?

A man from South Korea who played in 3 World Cups and in the English Premiere League once told me in his broken English, 'Before I have any money, I never worry about money. I get to the EPL and sign big contract, then all I think about is money.'

It is not our place to judge, but it is wise to learn from those who have come before us.

The scorecard society judges us by is tragically flawed, and pursuing it will leave you completely unfulfilled.

It is time we develop a new scorecard for how we define a truly successful life. I want you to think about a few people that you truly admire, and write out what characteristics they embodied that you would like to be known for."

John started to think about the people he truly admired, and he wrote down:

Courage
Boldness
Empathy
Loving
Grateful
Persistence
Joyful
Resourceful

Akira nodded. "Now I want you to choose the top four characteristics that are most important to you."

This was tough for John, because he felt like all of the characteristics on his list were really important. But he finally wrote down:

Boldness & Courage
Loving
Resourceful
Persistence

Akira smiled as the apprentices finished writing. "You now have your new scorecard. I want you to grade yourself twice a day on how you have done on the things that you have said are the most important characteristics for living a truly successful life. If you grade yourself around the middle of the day, then you will know what areas you need to focus on that evening. With this new scorecard, you can use any situation you find yourself in as an opportunity to grow these characteristics!"

John took a blank 4x6 note card as they were being passed around, and wrote out his new scorecard. He was excited because he now had a very practical tool for using any circumstance as an opportunity to develop into the man he wanted to become.

11

Evil's Best Weapon

One summer day, the weather was so hot and humid the sensei actually told the apprentices to stop chopping wood and carrying water an hour early, in order for everyone to spend some time in the nearby lake.

On the way to the water, Akira asked John if anyone had told him the story *Evil's Best Weapon*. John said that no one had, and Akira smiled wide, "Then you are in for a treat!"

As they walked, he began his story. "One day, an evil old witch was going out of business, and she had a yard sale to sell her potions and tools. You could buy all the traditional tools you think of when you think of evil: jealousy, anger, lust, pride, envy, deceit, and adultery. Droves of people flocked to the sale and all her shiny tools were sold to the highest bidder.

Towards the end of the day, after all the tools had been well picked through, all that remained were a few trash heaps of old worn-out and broken tools. One gentleman dug through the scraps and found a tool that was very well worn, and looked like it was on its last leg. Hoping for a good deal, he brought it to the woman to ask how much it cost.

The old witch was startled. 'That tool is too valuable for me to sell, it is the only one I'm passing down to my niece. Give it back to me. It should not have been out here!'

Now the man was even more intrigued. 'But it's so worn, and yet you claim it is worth more than all these other shinier and newer tools. I must know what this tool is.'

The witch refused to tell him, and instead she pried it from his hands and asked him to leave. She took the old tool back and hid it in her house, and by the day's end, every other tool had been sold except for that one.

A few months later, the witch was on her deathbed. She called for her niece. Her niece was very angry she had sold all of her fancy tools.

'How could you sell all your tools and not pass them on to me?!' she shouted.

The old witch waited for her to calm down, and then told her to look under her bed. The niece looked under the bed but all she saw was an old, worn-out tool.

She was surprised. 'This?! This old thing is all you left me?!'

The old witch looked at her and said, 'Oh how naive you are, young child. *This tool is discouragement, and it is more powerful than all the other tools combined.* The best part is that most people never suspect that it comes from you. Discouragement will allow you to get to a person's heart when none of the other tools will, and once they become discouraged, they are putty in your hands. You can squash the most powerful of dreams, level the greatest of ideas, and ruin almost anything in the world without detection, all by using this tool to plant the seeds of discouragement.'

And with nothing but that single tool of discouragement, her niece went on to become one of the most powerful witches to ever live.

John, one of the most powerful forces you will face during your time here is discouragement. It can come in many different forms; sometimes it is the voice inside your head that says you aren't good enough, while other times it might come from giving your best and still not succeeding. Still other times it will creep in in ways you might not even be aware of. But make sure you always keep your guard up, and fuel your heart with encouragement."

John nodded, asking, "How do I fuel my heart?"

Akira smiled. "Good question. You fuel your heart with six things: what you watch, what you read, what you listen to, who you surround yourself with, how you talk to yourself, and what you visualize. Let me ask you a question: if you owned a Lamborghini, would you ever put water into the gas tank?"

John looked up in confusion. "Of course not! That would ruin the engine!"

"Exactly," Akira said, "But this is what most people do with their hearts. You and I were created just like that Lamborghini, but if we put the wrong fuel into the gas tank of our hearts, we won't run as we were intended to. We get frustrated and discouraged because we know deep down that we were created for so much more. You were created perfectly and meticulously for a purpose John, but if you put the wrong fuel into your gas tank, it is very easy to get discouraged and break down as you go through the journey of life."

12

What Went Well?

On one particularly tough day of training, John just couldn't seem to shoot as well as normal. His groupings were loose and unfocused, and he became mentally distracted by the fit of his new shooting guard. As he finished the day in frustration, Akira took him aside, and asked him how his day had been.

"Terrible! I couldn't focus, I got distracted by my new shooting guard, and my groupings weren't as tight as they needed to be. I feel like a failure."

Akira smiled, and shrugged. "I didn't ask how you shot John, but since you brought it up, *what did you do well in training?*"

John paused, thrown off. He struggled to think of a single positive take-away from the day's shooting. "Nothing. I did nothing well." He said discouraged.

"I have a very hard time believing that John." said Akira. "Why do you think it is so hard for you to think of what you did well?"

John shrugged, "I guess I don't think about it, because... I don't want to get a big head."

"Let me tell you something, John: *I do*."

John looked at his sensei in surprise and confusion, as Akira continued. "It is much easier for your brain to focus on the negatives, even if they are actually totally outweighed by the positives! Many people's confidence suffers, because they are more concerned with appearing to be humble, so they have been conditioned to tell really negative stories about themselves and their performance.

Now, there are people who have the reverse challenge and can't see their flaws, but far and away the bigger issue is people who lack confidence and who are highly critical of themselves. But let's be clear, negativity and a 'nothing I do is good enough' attitude is *not* humility. A much smarter man than I said, 'Humility is not thinking less of your self, but thinking of your self less.'[4]

Let me tell you a couple secrets about how our marvelous brains *actually* work John. Your memories are not created through your experiences, rather they are created through the stories you tell yourself and others about those experiences. So, if you leave a practice or a match and you tell everyone how poorly you played, and you focus on all your mistakes that is what your brain remembers. Most people undermine all the hard work they are putting in by telling really negative stories and blocking out all the growth that is happening." Akira smiled.

"What do you mean "blocking out?" Said John as his nose scrunched and his eyebrows furrowed inquisitively.

"Our brains are marvelous machines, John, which process around eleven million bits of information per second. But we are only *aware* of about forty of those bits. In other words you are only aware of .00000364 of what is *actually* happening around you! You and I block out 99.99999% of what

---

4 C.S. Lewis Quote

our brain is processing. So, if we want to change the way our brain scans the world and start to adopt a more beneficial reality and perspective, we must start by rewiring the way our brain scans the world around us."

"Well, that sounds incredibly challenging! How in the world do you do that?" asked John.

Akira handed him a small notepad and a pen. "By writing it down."

John flipped through the blank pages, as Akira went on, "I want you to do this after every shooting session. I want you to start by writing a *value statement* at the top. It should say, 'My value comes from who I am, *not* from what I do.' Then, follow that with a *growth mindset statement*. 'Anything that happens to me today is in my best interest and it's an opportunity to learn and grow.' Then, I want you to write out between fifteen to sixty-three specific things you did well."

John blinked, taken aback. "Whoa, that's a *lot! I think that might be impossible!"*

"Of course it *feels* that way! That's because you haven't yet trained your brain to think that way. Do you remember the first time you tried to make a left hand lay up in basketball?" Asked Akira.

John blushed and mumbled, "Yes, I was eleven years old, and I started to cry. Truthfully, I started balling and ran out of the gym. I thought guy who was training me was a huge jerk! But he made me keep doing it for months, often through crying fits of frustration."

"Sounds like a tough trainer. Did it get easier though?" Akira asked.

"Yes, eventually I became highly skilled with finishing with my left hand." Said John as a smile broke through and things clicked in his mind.

"In time this will get easier as you consistently force your brain to scan the world differently, but until then I encourage you to always keep going until you have at least fifteen things. If you decide to quit before fifteen, make sure you at least get two more than where you quit the day before. Remember, this is rewiring your brain. It is hard work, but it is very worth it." Said Akira.

One thing that might be helpful is to carry this notebook with you, and jot things down as you go through practice, your day, or during breaks in competition. You may not need to write them all the way out during competition or practice, but write down enough to remember when you complete your journal later in the day. And remember John, you have ignored what you have done well for a long time, while blowing your 'flaws' out of proportion. So, maybe for the next six months let's try and do the reverse. Let's ignore the 'flaws,' focus on finding what you did well and how you got better."

"That's helpful, actually. I think I can do that," said John.

"The next part of the journal is writing out two *areas for growth*, but you only get to write these down once you get to fifteen specific things you have done well. You only get two areas because it is hard to remember to focus on more than two at any one time. By writing down only two areas you can look back at yesterday's journal and know exactly what you need to focus on today during training. Finally, the last thing you write out is at least two things you *learned* today, because remember 'nothing is a test.' Everything is an opportunity to learn, but we need to actually focus on learning. Akira said with a big smile.

John, it takes a lot of discipline to stick with a 'what went well journal,' but it is a very rewarding exercise with far-reaching implications for your life! If you can't see what you do well, it is awful hard to encourage other people with what they do well."

John nodded, encouraged to try this new exercise. As soon as he got back to his room, he flipped open the notebook and began writing. When he had finished, his entry looked like this…

Worth Statement: *My value comes from who I am, NOT from what I do.*

Growth Mindset: *Anything that happens today is in my best interest. It is an opportunity to learn and grow.*

What Went Well: (Write out 15 **specific** things you did well today. Feel free to use examples of areas you got better in even if they weren't the very best you can are capable of.)

1. *I kept my stance solid for every shot*
2. *I caught myself wondering if I would be able to finish the practice. Started to talk to myself instead of listening to myself*
3. *I was intentional about treating the other apprentices very well even when I felt like they didn't deserve it*
4. *I chose to take deep breaths before I approached the firing line*
5. *I held my core stable and kept clean lines in my shooting form*
6. *I cleared my mind before each release and remembered to focus on controllables*
7. *I saw Katsuo shoot three tight groupings, but I chose not to compare and focused on my own shots*
8. *I chose to see myself being very strong even when I felt my shoulder shake on my last set of draws*
9. *When I got frustrated and wanted to give up, I reminded myself that I am building my own house*
10. *I started and finished my practice today without anyone forcing me*
11. *I kept my breathing slow and focused on the firing line*
12. *I remembered to keep visualizing each arrow hitting where I aimed it, even when my shots were off*
13. *I remembered to pause and settle my mind and breathe before each release*
14. *I encouraged the other apprentices by reminding them of what they were doing well*

15. I did a better job today of letting the negative thoughts fly on by and not give them power
16. I kept my releases easy and unconscious

Areas For Growth: (Formerly called "Weaknesses" but we are looking at them as growth opportunities now)

- Keeping my mind clear and focusing on my process even when I am distracted
- Staying present after a mistake and focusing on what I need to do NOW

What I Learned: (This can be something that you already know but learned the importance of again)

- I shoot tighter groupings when I remember to release my goals and focus on my controllables instead
- By focusing on what my fellow apprentices do well, it creates a much better energy and environment for growth and optimum performance.

13

Another year passed, and John kept growing and learning. Every morning he chopped wood, and every evening he carried water. His hands developed thick calluses, his arms grew stronger, and his movements became fluid and memorized as he brain wrapped intricate wires of muscle memory called *myelin*.

One night during the summer John and the Sensei didn't find any games they wanted to watch on TV, so they decided on the new *Karate Kid* movie starring Jaden Smith.

During a commercial break, Akira told John about his admiration for Jaden's father Will. In an interview, he once heard Will say, "Talent you have naturally. Skill is only developed by hours and hours and hours of beating on your craft." Will went on, "I have never considered myself particularly talented, but where I excel is ridiculous, sickening work ethic… there is no easy way around it, no matter how talented you are, your talent is going to fail you if you are not skilled."

John grew up watching reruns of *The Fresh Prince of Bel Air*, and he always considered Will Smith to be one of those talented people to whom everything just came naturally.

He asked Akira, "So do you think that someone like Will Smith really isn't that talented?"

His sensei replied, "I think he might have plenty of talent, but I think that his talent is overshadowed by his character. A wise man once told me, 'Talent without character is like an expensive, fast car with no gas. It is useless without the fuel that drives it[5].'"

John nodded, as Akira went on. "And while I do not know what anyone is *born* with, I do know that *none* of us know our potential. In fact, I would argue that your potential is much greater than you ever realize, but it will take incredible dedication and purposeful training to unlock it. Most people never realize their potential, because when things get hard, or they experience failure, they just quit. Most people settle for average and what comes easy. They never give their very, very best and exhaust themselves in order to protect their ego. They enjoy being able to say, 'I didn't even really try,' or 'I didn't really care.' Because if they did really give it their best, and still failed, that would be too much for their ego to handle."

John felt like he had just uncovered one of the greatest secrets to success. "I guess it makes sense now that you explain it like that, because with things like Instagram and YouTube we only see the most edited, Photoshopped version of people's lives. It *feels* like they wake up like that, but really everything is staged, they took fifty pictures, and highly edited the very best one. No one posts anything of them not looking their best."

Akira nodded his approval. "Exactly! Never forget, you do not shine under the bright lights; the bright lights only reveal your work in the dark. We get so used to seeing superstars on game day, that we forget what we do not see: all the hours they spend beating on their craft, drenched in sweat, at the point of exhaustion, with no one watching[6]. Too many people seek exposure from the bright lights, but the bright lights only expose their lack of faithfulness to their craft in the dark."

---

5   The wise man is Jon Gordon
6   This is from a note Anson Dorrance wrote Mia Hamm

14

Wandering Eyes

After that evening, John went to bed with a renewed sense of excitement to chop wood, carry water and beat on his craft. Over the next couple of months, he still had his days that were more challenging than others, but overall he was in a much better place.

Eventually though, John developed a wandering eye. One of his fellow apprentices, a young man named Katsuo, seemed to constantly be achieving things faster than John. His shots were stronger and more accurate, and he didn't complain or grow tired with his work. It seemed like he was always doing everything better than John.

And he wasn't the only one. John started looking at all of his friends, and began to grow jealous at how easy things seemingly came for them and how hard things were for him.

One day, John was walking to lunch when Akira came up beside him. "Why the heavy shoulders John? It looks like something is really weighing on you."

John sulked, "I have really been struggling the last few months, because it just feels like it's not fair that I work so hard, yet other people who are more talented than me continue to surpass me with less effort. Do you know how embarrassing it is to be busting my butt every day, and giving my everything to get better, and it never feels good enough? I watch Katsuo give half the effort, and he's still better than me. I just feel like I should quit, go home, and get a normal job. Maybe becoming a samurai archer just isn't for me."

Akira stopped, spun John around by his shoulders and stared deep into his soul with his piercing grey eyes. "Let me tell you a story, John. When I was your age, I was the last in my class in *everything*. I struggled. I wanted to quit. I was constantly embarrassed, because I gave everything, but it never felt good enough."

"So how did you get so good?" John said.

"I never gave up, and I realized the whole time I was building my own house. A sensei shared with me that very same story about Kota building his own house, and I realized that it wasn't about what I was doing, but rather about who I became. John, let me tell you two very important things: comparison is the thief of all joy, and the grass isn't greener on the other side. *The grass is greener where you water it.* You have grown up in a society where things like social media and twenty-four hour television have established a culture that is hyper-focused on comparison. But if you are constantly comparing, you will have all the joy sucked out of you. You must focus on *your* journey, yours alone."

If you don't, you risk not only losing your joy, but losing any chance of *true* success in the long run. Comparison is incredibly short-sighted, and if we focus only on the successes of others, we do it at our own expense. As a great writer[7] once said, 'There is nothing noble in being superior to your fellow man; true nobility is being superior to your former self.' The person who chops wood & carries water no matter if up by 20 points or down by 20 points crushes the field in the long run, but more importantly crushes the version of themselves focused on just winning. It's worthless compar-

---

7 Ernest Hemingway

ing to others, the real comparison is to ourselves. Which philosophy, belief, or mindset, is most beneficial to you over the long haul? Are you playing the short game or the long game? Compare yourself and measure yourself compared only to your own potential, not to that of your competition or your teammates."

He continued, stern. "If it rains, bottle the water and sell it. If crap falls from the sky, package it and sell fertilizer. If it is sunny, plant a garden. Use what *you and you alone* have been given. You do not know what other people are going through, and *everyone* has their own unique struggles, even Katsuo. Stop trying to live their life, because there are millions of people who would give anything to live your life. Did you know there are a billion people without access to clean drinking water, and millions of people with debilitating diseases and accidents that have left them nearly paralyzed?"

John perked up and he got tears in his eyes as he thought about Jordan. He would give anything for the opportunity John was complaining about. "I guess I got so distracted with the people who seemingly have more than me, that I forgot about those with less than me."

"You must always keep perspective, John. It is very easy to lose it, and when you lose perspective you forget that this life is but a vapor; we are here today and gone tomorrow. Do not waste your life, John. Focus on what truly matters, and do not fall for the lies of the comparison thief."

"I want you to try an exercise I do every morning in the shower that helps me shift from comparison to a heart posture of gratitude. I call it gratefulness meditation. I want you to sit down in the shower for five to ten minutes every morning and start by thanking God for everything you can think of. I usually start with the little things that are so easy to take for granted, like clean drinking water, the ability to walk, talk, and feed myself. I even thank Him for all the doors that have closed in my life. Eventually, I just slip into a meditative state and try to just observe my thoughts that fly through my mind without judging them. If I have a tough day I will usually visualize whatever challenges are likely to arise, and then I see myself overcoming them and being at my very best."

John had a puzzled look on his face.

"I know it sounds strange, but I have been doing it for over three decades, and it works." Said Akira.

"Ok, ok, I promise to try it out for at least two weeks and then I will let you know how it goes!"

15

Rough Side of the Mountain

O ne day, just as the apprentices reached the shooting range, the sky cracked with thunder, and began pouring down rain like John had never seen before. Everyone was instructed to go into the dining hall. Once they arrived, they were asked to be seated.

Up on the board was written: *Talent vs. Skill.*

As the apprentices settled in, Akira began to teach, speaking about how the difference between talent and skill is widely misunderstood. "Many people think that all you need is talent, and that only the chosen few can ever truly succeed. Many talented people believe the same thing, and then get frustrated when they fail, because they think all they need to do is show up, and everything will magically line up for them because of their talent."

After everyone was dismissed, John waited around to talk with the old sensei.

John was bubbling over with excitement. "As you were talking, I remembered that Michael Jordan got cut from his high school basketball team. He even had a commercial once where he said, 'Maybe it's my fault. Maybe I led you to believe that basketball was a God-given gift, and not something that I worked for every single day of my life.' Many people thought the commercial was M. J. going after LeBron James, and sure enough,

LeBron's work ethic and willingness to sacrifice increased dramatically since that commercial. It wasn't until he had that shift that he actually won an NBA championship."

"Very interesting," mused Akira. "I didn't know that, but it doesn't surprise me. I always wondered what happened, but I had never heard that commercial or M. J. quote before. Maybe it did have something to do with LeBron's shift in mentality and work ethic."

It was still pouring rain outside, so Akira asked John if he wanted to join him by the fire. John agreed, loading a few logs into the furnace. They sat, enjoying the warmth of the flames in the chilly dining hall.

Akira asked, "John, you love golf, don't you?"

John replied, "Yes! Absolutely, my dad, Jordan and I grew up playing every Friday, and it developed a special bond between us. Jordan LOVED to watch us play!"

The old man smiled as John spoke of the warm memories he and his family shared on the course. Finally he asked, "But do you know the story of how golf balls were first made?"

"I don't think I do," John realized.

Akira continued, "At first, golf balls were made smooth, without any dimples at all. But eventually during testing, one man started to notice something strange. He developed a theory about it, and one day he came into work early to test his theory, because he thought that everyone would think he was crazy if he shared his theory with them.

His theory was that the golf balls that had been hit many times, the bruised and rough ones, actually traveled much further than the perfectly smooth ones did. Sure enough, he was right: these tiny imperfections create a thin layer of turbulence around the ball, reducing drag and allowing air to flow further and more smoothly around the ball. And that is why today, all golf balls have dimples on them.

John, I know you are afraid of your perceived weaknesses and shortcomings, and you feel like your journey has always taken you up the rough side of the mountain. But when you don't give up and you don't give in, the rough side of the mountain actually molds you and shapes you into a person who can travel much further in life, just like those roughed-up golf balls. The blemishes, scars, and setbacks are what give you the character to take you places other people are too soft and smooth to go!"

John nodded, feeling a weight lift gently off his shoulders as Akira spoke.

"Are you still struggling with comparing yourself to other people who things come more easily to?" his sensei asked.

"I'm doing a lot better since I started doing the gratefulness mediation every morning, but it is still hard at times."

"I think talent is often more of a curse than a blessing, John. Did you know that most people who win the lottery are worse off financially five years down the road than they were before winning the lottery?"

John shook his head. "I never knew that."

"Winning the lottery skips the valuable process of going up the rough side of the mountain. Instead of being forced to learn and develop the skills necessary for creating or sustaining success, you arrive at the top, without any of what it takes to stay there. Talent can be a kind of lottery, John. A talented athlete is often less likely to develop the skills and work ethic that a less-talented one has to develop just to survive, and because of that, they may end up much worse off down the road. They never learned the work ethic, persistence, and grit needed to overcome the inevitable challenges that life throws their way.

Remember, greatness isn't for the chosen few, but for the few who consistently and persistently choose.

I know that it seems like life is unfair right now, and you want things to be easier, but the rough side of the mountain will actually prepare you for life much better than the smooth side. Believe it or not, the setbacks of today can quickly become the forging blades of greatness for tomorrow. In fact, a wise man once said, "hardship often prepares ordinary people for an extraordinary destiny.[8]"

"Wow, I'd never thought of it that way before," John pondered. "I guess I need to rethink my setbacks! Thank you so much for sharing your wisdom and perspective. I'm not sure I would have made it this long without you."

Akira just smiled, nodding patiently. "My blessing!"

---

8 The wise man was C.S. Lewis

16

Harnessing Power

One evening John and Akira had gone on a long walk after dinner to the edge of the property to catch the sunset. As they watched the sun drop to the horizon, Akira pointed to a large oak tree, which had been uprooted and lay fallen at the edge of the property.

He asked, "Do you see that tree, John?"

"Of course. What happened to it?"

"A very strong wind storm blew it over, many years ago. But after that same windstorm, a company in the city came out and set up those. Do you know that they are?"

Akira pointed in the other direction, across a wide field. Far away, John could glimpse the spinning turbines of a wind farm.

"A wind farm?"

"Exactly. Isn't it strange, John, that wind can be both creative and destructive at the same time? It all depends on how you harness it. It can destroy homes or trees, or it can create power or push a sailboat across an ocean."

John nodded, "I'd never thought of it that way."

Akira continued, "Words are a lot like that. Just like the wind, they are everywhere. We use them every day to talk to others, but most importantly, we use them to talk to *ourselves*. And just like the wind, their power can either destroy, or create. You may not have control over how other people talk to you, but you do have control over how you talk to yourself. And that is hugely important, because…

Words put pictures in your mind.
Pictures in your mind impact how you feel.
How you feel impacts what you do.
What you habitually do impacts your destiny.

What amazes me is that many people, often without realizing it, use this power to talk themselves into choices that are harmful for themselves in the long run, even if they might offer temporary happiness. Or, they use their words to give power to their inner critic, destroying their own joy and growth before it even has a chance to start."

"What do you mean?" asked John.

"We are all experts in mental training, John, because we practice it every day. Most people just aren't aware of it. Our brains can't distinguish between what is real and imagined, and we can actually wrap muscle memory with vivid visualization. You use visualization every single day, though you might only be using it in negative ways."

"How so?" asked John.

"Do you ever worry, John? Worrying is a form of negative visualization, that helps create the scenario you see happening in your mind. The hard choice, but the one that is best for us in the long run, is to use our words to put positive pictures in our minds, and to talk to ourselves in ways that push us toward growth and toward what is most beneficial for ourselves in the long run. It might sound crazy at first, but using beneficial and constructive self-talk instead of giving power to our inner critic is one of the most formidable strategies possible to use toward reaching our own potential.

You might not be able to stop negative thoughts or your inner critic from screaming at you, but you don't have to believe them, and you can definitely talk to yourself rather than just listening to the negativity!"

John nodded, understanding. "Just like the wind?"

Akira smiled, "Yes, John. Just like the wind."

17

Diet Coke

One night John was watching TV alone, when a commercial came on. It was a loud, garish advertisement for a product that promised its users they could lose twenty pounds in two weeks. Suddenly, a voice sounded from behind him...

"What a ridiculous idea!"

John whirled in surprise to find Akira standing at the doorway. The sensei entered the room, shaking his head.

"Those commercials always frustrate me and remind me of something. Have you ever seen a person order a two or three thousand calorie meal, complete with a huge dessert, but then ask for a Diet Coke? What is that Diet Coke possibly doing for them? It might make them feel better, but it is not helping them get better! Unfortunately, this is how most people treat mental training."

Sensing John's confusion, Akira explained, "Most people want to consume whatever they want to for 86,000 seconds of their day, just like they want to eat what they want to eat for most of each day. But then, just like this commercial offers a 'get fit quick' fix for a fat body, they want a trick they can do for the other 400 seconds left in their day that is going to override all the negative training they've been doing all day long!"

John nodded, understanding, as Akira went on.

"Mental training is not magic. It is deliberate, intentional, and extremely hard training. If I told you it would be easy to lose one hundred fifty pounds, you would think I was crazy, just like you do when you watch these commercials. It is the same with mental training and developing true mental toughness. It's not sexy, it's dirty, hard work."

The commercial ended, and John smiled. "So you're sure I can't lose twenty pounds in two weeks?"

Akira just looked at John's athletic frame and smiled back, "If you lost twenty pounds, what would be left?"

18

The Path to Mastery

Even though John enjoyed his time with Akira, it took four very long and very frustrating years before he was able to move up from the seven-foot target to the full targets more than a hundred feet away.

When the day finally came, John couldn't wait. He walked to the firing line filled with confidence, drawing his arrow smoothly and quickly. With a smile, he released it... only to watch in total disappointment as it flew sideways, <u>totally off-target</u>.

He couldn't believe it! He'd been shooting every day for four years, and now the bow and arrow felt like foreign objects in his hands. Once again, he wondered if all this time had been a waste.

For weeks, he couldn't hit the target. Every day he tried, and every day his arrows flared all over the place. Then one day, Akira went over to check on his progress.

John shrugged in total discouragement. "I can't hit the target, and I feel like giving up. Maybe I'm just not meant to be a samurai archer!"

John expected Akira to respond with some of his usual words of wisdom, but instead the old sensei beckoned John to follow him. He walked away from the firing line, to a patch of dirt. He bent down, and used an arrow to draw something in the dirt.

John peered at the drawings curiously. They looked like this:

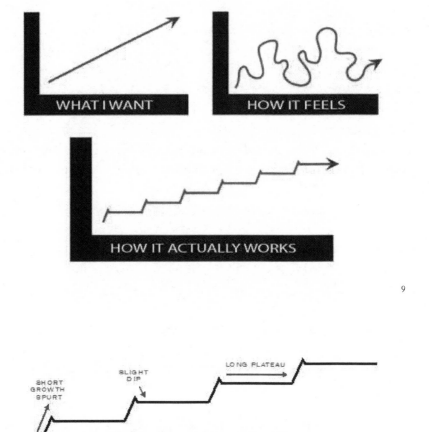

WHAT I WANT

HOW IT FEELS

HOW IT ACTUALLY WORKS

9

SHORT GROWTH SPURT

SLIGHT DIP

LONG PLATEAU

THE PATH TO MASTERY

---

9 The bottom illustration is "The Path to Mastery" as George Leonard explains in his book, *Mastery*

"What is that?"

"That," replied Akira, "Is the path to mastery."

He explained that while John wanted to feel constant improvement, mastery moves much differently: it moves in steps, not constants. So while John might feel discouraged now, he was on a long plateau, and in time he would eventually have another growth spurt.

But John was tired of all the philosophical sayings and stories, and he couldn't believe the words that slipped out of his mouth. "You make it sound so easy, but I bet you can't even hit the target any more, *old man*!"

Akira calmly responded, "Meet me back here at ten tonight."

19

I Aim with Everything

All day long, John couldn't shake his nerves. He knew he shouldn't have spoken to any sensei that way, but especially not the one who had invested so much time and energy in him. John was fearful of what would come next. Half expecting to be beaten, John showed up at the shooting range a few minutes early to scout the scene.

At 9:59, Akira walked up silently, holding his bow and two arrows. John was confused, because it was pitch black outside. You could barely see to walk. But Akira calmly walked over to one of the shooting blocks, nocked an arrow, and drew his bow.

John watched in awe, as — all at once, with intense focus that still seemed effortless somehow — Akira exhaled and released.

THWACK!

John knew that sound. Akira had hit the target, but it seemed impossible.

Once again, the old man nocked his arrow, drew it, and...

THWACK!

This time, the noise wasn't as loud, but John knew it must have hit something. He took off running to the target, and when he got there he couldn't believe his eyes.

It seemed impossible. Akira's first arrow was lodged in the middle of the target, while his second had hit the first arrow, splitting it in half.

John walked back stunned, stuttering, "How on earth did you do that? It's impossible!"

Akira smiled, pointing down in the dirt to where his drawings were still clear. With nothing but a little bit of moonlight he indicated the steps of the final drawing. "Many years of chop wood, carry water."

He indicated the bottom step. "First year, you must learn to aim with your eyes."

He indicated the next step. "Second year, you must learn to draw your bow smoothly, hold it stable, and aim with your muscles."

Again, the next step. "Third year, you must learn to breathe slowly, control your diaphragm, and aim with your lungs."

He repeated this, all the way to the top of the drawing, where he stopped. "John, I have been chopping wood and carrying water for forty-nine years. And while you may only aim with your eyes and your muscles and your lungs right now, I aim with *everything*. The way I stand, the position of my feet, how much tension I put in the bow, how much tension I have in my hands, how I breathe, and what I see in my mind all impact the end result. Everything impacts everything. Everything is aiming.

You have much to learn, John. Get some sleep, and tomorrow we chop wood, carry water."

John just nodded in total amazement, thankful for such a masterful and patient teacher.

20

Bamboo

The next morning at breakfast, Akira told John to meet him at the big bamboo grove in ten minutes. Still mesmerized from the night before, John quickly agreed.

When John arrived seven minutes later, Akira was already there waiting for him. "Let's go for a walk. I want to tell you a story," he said. John replied, "First, I owe you an apology. I am very sorry for speaking to you in such a disrespectful manner. It was wrong, and I am very sorry."

The old man looked at John and said with a smile, "I appreciate that you recognized this on your own, and I accept your apology. Now, has anyone ever told you the story of bamboo, John?"

He pointed to the towering grove of bamboo trees, with their thick green trunks and whispering leaves. John shook his head, "No, sir."

"Well then, you are in for a treat!" Akira grinned and went on, "You see, many people love bamboo. They love the bamboo trees, and they love the bamboo wood, but very few people understand the process of growing bamboo. You dig up the soil and make sure it is good soil, and then you plant the bamboo seed. You then must faithfully water it every day. After three months, guess what starts to happen?"

John said excitedly, "The bamboo tree starts to sprout up out of the ground?"

"Nothing! You see absolutely nothing happening. You keep watering it and watering it, but you continue to see nothing happening for one year, then two years, then three years. Do you know what happens after three years, John?"

John replied, more tentatively this time, "The bamboo tree starts to sprout up out of the ground?"

"Nothing! You see absolutely nothing."

John shook his head, "I don't understand."

"What you don't see happening is what is taking place *beneath the surface*. Beneath the surface, a massive, dense foundation of roots is spreading out all throughout the ground to prepare for the rapid growth that the bamboo will experience. So, you keep watering it and watering it, and eventually, after *five* years of seeing nothing at all happen above the surface, the bamboo tree shoots up to over ninety feet tall in just six weeks!

You see John, most people want the ninety-foot-tall bamboo tree without the five years of the *process*. They want the bamboo to grow to ninety feet tall in six weeks, but without the five years of invisible growth, the bamboo wouldn't have a solid foundation, and it could never sustain the massive and rapid growth that occurs. This is why you see people who achieve massive levels of 'success' end up broke, homeless and divorced. Did you know that around 75% of NFL players and around 65% of NBA players end up bankrupt, homeless, and divorced?"

Shaken, John shook his head no.

"Do you remember when I told you that the majority of people who win the lottery end up worse off financially than they were before winning the lottery, just five years down the road?"

John nodded, of course he remembered.

"John, chopping wood and carrying water is the price of admission for the opportunity to reach sustained excellence. Like the roots of a bamboo tree, it is a long and arduous process of invisible growth, where you are building the foundation that is necessary to sustain success. For many years it might feel as if nothing is happening, but you must trust the process and continue to chop wood and carry water, day in day out, regardless of what is happening around you.

There will be distractions. There will be people who tell you that you are stupid or crazy for doing it. There will be people who try and lure you off the path with quick fixes and get rich quick schemes. But you must be wise and stay the path, and continue to build your foundation by chopping wood and carrying water every day. Greatness isn't sexy John, it is the dirty, hard work that is often very boring. You have a bright future, but you must walk a dark and often lonely path, and never forget --"

"I know, I know," interrupted John. "No matter what happens, I must chop wood, and carry water."

Akira couldn't help but grin. "You have learned much, but you still have much to learn."

21

Road Signs on the Path to Mastery

On a beautiful fall day while John was out training, Akira sat nearby, watching as John shot arrow after arrow. Eventually, he grabbed two cups of water and handed one to John.

"Time for a break, John."

John was happy to oblige, and they sat in silence for a minute. Then, Akira said, "Have I told you lately that I love to watch you shoot, and that I am very proud of you?"

John's face turned a little red as he replied, "Yes, you tell me every week."

"Good!" Akira nodded. "Did you know that I drove trucks all over Asia for two years when I was in my early twenties?"

"Really?! I didn't know they even had cars back then!"

John grinned at his own joke as Akira shook his head, "I'm not *that* old, John. Need I remind you about our night of shooting in the dark?"

John laughed, "Of course not, I'll never forget it!"

"The interesting thing about driving trucks back then, was that without navigational technology, we depended a lot on road signs to help us. You would often snap out of haze and wonder, 'Wait a minute, am I going in the right direction?!!'"

He looked off for a minute, then continued:

"The same thing often happens with people in their teams, businesses, corporations, and families. The road signs on the path to mastery are similar regardless of the context we find ourselves in at any particular time in life. We can take solace in knowing that we are going in the right direction by the signs on the road. Here are some of those road signs:

- This is hard.
- I don't feel like doing _____ today.
- Everyone else has more time than me.
- I don't feel like this is making a difference.
- Almost no one else is doing this.

Sound familiar?

The thing about all of these signs is that they provide information, but they don't give a whole lot of instruction. Instead, they are more like the mile-markers or rest stop signs that tell us where things are. But the great thing about most highways is that they don't just provide *information*; they actually provide *instruction* that will help us move safely and efficiently towards our destination. These are the yellow diamond signs that we see instructing us about a speed change for a sharp bend, uneven roads, or road work ahead. The road signs on the path to mastery are no different. So, what are some of the path to mastery's instructions?

- *Talk to yourself instead of listening to yourself.*
- *Ask the question, "What is one thing I can do to make the situation better?" rather than, "why is this happening to me?"*
- *Live by principles rather than feelings.*

Finally, there are warning signs that mark the path. They are signs that warn us about the result of our choices. On the highway we see warnings about fines in a work zone, fines for littering, and fines for HOV violators. They are the boundaries that we must operate in, or else there will be a consequence. The path to mastery is marked with those as well.

- *Your choice creates your challenge*
- *You are building your own house*
- *Your choice creates a challenge for those on your team*
- *You will reap what you sow*
- *The grass is greener where you water it*
- *The wise man finds the diamonds on his own land*

Even though the path to mastery is available to everyone, very few will choose to take it.

Will there be obstacles? *Yes.*
Will there be people who try to hold you back? *Yes.*
Will there be circumstances that create
challenges outside of your control? *Yes.*
Will it be lonely at times? *Yes.*

But choosing to believe that anything that happens is in your best interest will turn all of the challenges and circumstances into a refinery that will shape your character and skills, and will develop within you an ability to change the world."

John nodded, amazed. Then, a smile grew on his face as he began to laugh.

"Is something funny, John?"

He looked at his sensei and grinned, "Sure is. I just pictured you in a trucker hat!"

Akira began to laugh as well. "Aren't you glad I didn't stick to trucking? I know I am."

Be Where Your Feet Are

A few more years passed, and John had begun to hit the far target with some consistency, becoming more and more accurate. His excitement grew, because the annual apprentice tournament was coming up, and he felt like it would finally be his time to shine and prove to everyone how good he had become.

But that week, John really began to struggle with a concept he had just learned in training. A sensei had talked about the need to be fully absorbed in the moment. The way he described it, it was almost as if the greatest samurai archers arrived at a place where they were so fully absorbed in the moment that they melded with the bow and arrow, so that they were no longer two separate things, but became one.

It reminded John of a concept he had been taught at a basketball mental skills workshop in high school. The teacher had shared the importance of *playing present*. He told John that the majority of people feel pressure and never come close to playing to their potential, because they never *play present*[10]. Instead, they play in the past or the future, which is where they feel pressure. There is no such thing as pressure in the present moment.

John didn't understand how to play present, but had made a commitment to himself to try to learn how. He had even reached out to a few

---

10 This concept was originated by Graham Betchart

people on Twitter, trying to discover how to be more effective at playing present.

His favorite response said simply, "Sit in the front row away from friends and teammates, turn off your phone, and take notes by hand, for every class."

One afternoon, John was so absorbed with thinking this through, that he nearly ran headfirst into a tree on his way to the shooting range. Stumbling, he caught himself, as…

"Good catch, I thought you were going down!" It was Akira, who had seen the whole thing and couldn't help but let out a belly laugh. John joined in, red with embarrassment, as Akira continued, "What are you thinking about? It must be something big, if you're walking into trees thinking about it!"

John started explaining how confused he was by the concept of playing present. He shared that favorite response from years ago about sitting in the front row.

Akira nodded, quizzical. "So, did you do what he told you to do?"

John squirmed a bit, mumbling something indiscernible.

Akira said, "I didn't think you had, or you wouldn't be struggling with the concept. Here is what you must understand: to play present, you must first learn to *live* present. Remember, you are always training!"

John nodded, realizing something: "I'm also late. Now I have to go chop wood, carry water!" He bowed to his sensei and turned to leave, but Akira wasn't finished.

"Excuse me?" he said. "John, there is only one thing you *have to* do in life, and that is die. You are always doing what you *want to* do, because there is *always* a choice. You may not like the choices, or the consequences, but you always have a choice. When you tell yourself that you *have to* do something, it creates a negative internal energy, but when you realize you *want to* do something it creates a more beneficial internal energy."

John nodded, "Then let me correct myself: I *want to* go chop wood, carry water now!"

Akira smiled, watching his apprentice go, proud of how John had transformed.

23

Goal vs. Mission

The day before the big apprentice tournament, John was on a walk with Akira.

"How are you feeling about the tournament?" Akira asked.

"Great! I put in my work in the dark, and now it's my time to shine under the bright lights. My goal is to win the tournament, and I think I finally have the skill to accomplish that," John said with excitement.

Akira pondered that for a silent moment, then replied, "Do you know why so many people love goals, John? Because they secretly let them off the hook. If your goal is to become a doctor, there are a lot of people who can stop that from happening. There are many checkpoints along the way where people can tell you that you aren't smart enough, or that you don't qualify. But if you look at Mother Theresa's mission, 'to serve the needs of the sick and the dying,' no one could ever stop her from living that out.

Goals actually allow you to shirk responsibility. But a mission? Only the person in the mirror can stop you from living that out.

I think one of the reasons so many young people today are floundering around chasing all the wrong things, is because they are bored with goals. They need a compelling mission. One hundred years ago, teen-agers were leading armies, raising families, and living inspired lives. They might have lived 'boring' lives by today's standards, but I would argue many of them were inspired by a compelling mission from a very young age. Today, our parents and coaches do all sorts of things to shelter kids from the consequences of their choices, and rarely inspire them with a mission.

I believe a mission is something you can do right where you are, anywhere, using only what you have. You do not need anyone's permission.

So, what is your mission John? It is much deeper than a goal, and it is okay to borrow one from others and then refine it as you go. But your mission will act as your internal navigation system. Without a mission, you will flounder through life and very easily end up with your ladder on the 'oh sh**' building."

John was surprised, but couldn't help cracking up. "What building is that?" he asked.

"Many people keep climbing and climbing, only to get to the end of their life and the top of the ladder, and realize their ladder has been on the wrong building. Without a mission, it is easy to lose perspective on what truly matters. A mission will make you think beyond the moment, which is greatly important because the only thing that is significant about the moment is who you become in the process, and the impact you have on others.

No one on their death bed is worried about how they did in a game, on a test, or how much money they made. They care about their relationships, and who they have become as a person. I know that in the moment, the achievements feel like a big deal, but with perspective, you will realize just how insignificant they really are."

John nodded, but in all honesty, his mind was still set on the tournament the next day.

"Do you understand what I mean?" asked Akira. John said he did, but Akira knew better: John's mind was elsewhere. He sighed, knowing what was coming, but knowing that he had to let John experience it on his own.

Oftentimes, failure is the greatest teaching tool.

24

Surrender

Sure enough, when the tournament came around, John just couldn't seem to per-form as well as he knew he could. Anxiety got the best of him, and after blowing his first three rounds, he wasn't even close to hitting the target by the end of it.

So instead of winning, or even placing, he watched in jealousy as Katsuo's arrows slammed into the bullseye, winning him the tournament.

As John walked off, emotion overcame him like a tidal wave, and tears of pure frustration began to fall. He had worked so hard for the last six years, and now he felt like he was back at square one, shooting at a seven-foot target. Lost in frustration, he walked for miles, ending up at the edge of the community's property. He collapsed at the top of a beautiful overlook, exhausted. He was so worn out, that he eventually dozed off.

A while later, a familiar voice roused him...

"John?" Sure enough, it was Akira. He offered John a bottle of water and a sandwich. "I figured you might be here."

The old man gestured to the surrounding hills, rolling in miles in every direction. "When I was an apprentice, I too used to come up here when I was frustrated with my training."

John began to eat and drink, as Akira continued, "John, I knew this was going to happen. As soon as you told me your goal was to win the tournament last week, I knew you had allowed your focus to shift away from the process and onto the uncontrollables. You cannot play present if you are focused on winning or the outcome."

As the sun began to set, the sky ignited with an explosion of color. Akira looked John in the eyes. "I want you to do something for me, John. I want you to go for a two minute gratefulness walk. I want you to walk around for two minutes thanking God for everything you are grateful for, and make sure you pay special attention to all the little things you often take for granted."

John nodded, deciding to give it a shot. After two minutes, he returned with a huge smile on his face. "That was amazing! I could feel the energy inside of me shift!"

Akira nodded, "Remember that the next time you are struggling and you need a perspective shift! It's not just what you do, but it is also the heart posture you have while doing it. If you broke your legs, I bet you would give anything to just be able to go for a walk. But it is easy to lose perspective and focus on silly things like the results of a tournament, rather than on being grateful for even being able to participate in that tournament in the first place.

When you operate with a heart posture of gratefulness, you free yourself up to be at your best and slip into the zone. Not to mention, you are also much more of a joy to be around for those you love."

John nodded, as he took in the sunset. Akira thought for a minute, then said, "John, I want to share with you the most important piece of wisdom my sensei ever shared with me.

The ultimate illusion of the human experience is control[11]. The person you want beside you in battle is the guy who has surrendered the outcome, and surrendered to the fact that he might die. When you surrender the outcome, you are freed up to be at your best, to be in the moment, and to trust your training. It is the one who has surrendered the outcome who ironically has the greatest chance of survival.

It is the one who has surrendered the outcome who has the greatest chance of success. It is the one who has surrendered to the fact that he could fail, who has the greatest likelihood of not failing. Until you surrender the outcome, you will always be the greatest enemy to your own success. In order to reach your greatest potential you must operate with a heart posture of gratitude, <u>commit </u>to the controllables, <u>surrender </u>the outcome, and <u>trust </u>the process."

Surrendering the outcome doesn't mean you care less about the outcome or your process. It doesn't mean you don't give your very best. It simply means that you have surrendered the outcomes that are outside of your control. Many mornings I pray and surrender things that I desperately want to control, but know I don't have control over. Surrendering the outcome is about having peace with that which is outside of our control without sacrificing the effort or care of what is inside of our control."

---

11 Judah Smith quote

25

Famous Failures

The week after the tournament, the community buzzed because of a special guest they were hosting for the week. Jackie Chan was going to be arriving later that day and speaking to the group that night, and John couldn't be more excited to get to meet him.

When Jackie got up to speak, he said he wanted to talk to them about the importance of failure, and that failure can be an incredible launching pad if you have a growth mindset. He said that a growth mindset is believing that, "anything that happens to me is in my best interest and is an opportunity to learn and grow."

Mr. Chan began to share a list of people who became famous after persevering through many continuous failures:

"It was 1937 when Theodore Geisel's first book hit the market after being rejected twenty-six times by different publishers. He went on to write a few books you might have read, such as *Cat In The Hat*, *Green Eggs and Ham*, and *Oh The Places We Will Go*.

Einstein's teachers labeled him 'mentally slow.' He didn't speak until almost five years old, and he was expelled from school.

Ben Carson was told he was stupid by teachers, and made to sit in the back corners of classrooms. He eventually became the first neurosurgeon to ever separate Siamese twins attached at the skull.

Oprah was fired and told she was 'unfit for television.'

David Sanders' famous chicken recipes were rejected by over 1,000 different restaurants, but you have probably eaten at a *KFC*.

A young engineer named Soichiro wanted a certain engineering job at *Toyota*, and he was very upset he didn't get it. So, he left and started a brand using his last name: *Honda*.

Henry had multiple businesses fail under his leadership, but eventually he created a little company called *Ford*.

Walt was fired from a local Kansas City newspaper for 'lacking creativity' and 'having no original ideas.' *Mr. Disney's* original ideas still draw billions to his amusement parks and movies every single year.

At thirty years old Steve was fired from the company he created, until *Apple* begged him to come back and save the company ten years later.

Tom was told he was 'too stupid to learn anything' but Mr. Edison did invent the first light bulb along with at least *one thousand and ninety-three* other things.

Their group was told they 'have no future in show business' but I bet the person who told *The Beatles* that might have eventually found himself with no future in show business.

Steven was rejected from the University of Southern California three times, and eventually dropped out of another college. He created a few movies you might have seen like *Jaws*, *Jurassic Park*, and *Indiana Jones*.

Rowland Hussey had seven straight businesses fail before he started *Macy's*.

A young singer named Paul's sample tape was continuously rejected by record labels as, 'not suitable for us,' but those same companies perked up their ears when *Bono* and his band *U2* eventually became some of the most successful rock stars of all time.

Akio's company was so broke they started making rice cookers that didn't work very well at all, but after many years of barely keeping the lights on, *Sony* found their niche.

Winston failed the sixth grade and was beaten in every election he partook in, until becoming the prime minister. His last name, *Churchill*, is now synonymous with the stalwart leadership that helped the Allies defeat Hitler in World War II.

Abraham failed at seemingly everything he put his hand to (including multiple businesses and runs at office) but *President Lincoln* eventually got a couple things right, like saving the Union and the Emancipation Proclamation.

Jerry froze his first time up on the big stage, and was consequently booed off it. His television show 'about nothing' was laughed at and ridiculed, until *Seinfield* became one of the longest-running and most popular shows in television history.

Vincent only sold one painting during his lifetime and was a true starving artist, but today *Van Gogh's* paintings together are worth billions.

Mr. Presley was fired from the Grand Old Opry in Nashville and told to 'go back to driving a truck.' *Elvis* was able to buy many trucks in his lifetime while selling a couple records along the way.

A shoe company was on the brink of bankruptcy for over a decade before they really took off, and NIKE is still doing pretty well to this day.

Ludwig was completely deaf, which made playing the violin and composing pretty difficult. Apparently a few people still play *Beethoven's* music today."

Jackie Chan paused, every eye in the room locked on him.

He continued, "I'm grateful these people didn't give up, and I hope you don't give up either. Because your failures, shortcomings, and challenges can either end up as your *excuse* or your *story*. I hope you choose courage, curiosity, and persistence. Because those are stories worth telling."

Having watched all of Jackie's films with his father and Jordan growing up, John was a huge fan. But it wasn't his movies that John was still thinking about that night as he lay in bed. Instead, it was the incredible stories Jackie told; John never realized that so many of the people he admired had gone through such adversity throughout their lives.

As he finally drifted off to sleep, he knew that if all of them could overcome such incredible challenges, then so could he.

26

The illusion of partially controllable goals

One day, as the sun was about to go down, Akira found John at the shooting range. He was still firing, intensely focused. THWACK! THWACK! THWACK! He sent arrow after arrow into the target, hurriedly reloading and moving on to the next.

Akira calmly asked, "John, what are you shooting for?"

"I need to get four bullseye groupings in a row before I lose the light."

"Why?"

Without thinking, John snapped, "Because that's Katsuo's record, and I need to beat him!"

"Be honest. Do you really *need* to do that?"

John shook his head, slowly deflating, as Akira continued…

"John, let me tell you story about trying to reach a goal before losing the light. A very long time ago, I was in love with a girl named Kimiko. One summer, I surprised her with a trip to a land she had always wanted to visit: Croatia, home of some of the world's most beautiful waterfalls.

There was one waterfall in particular whose beauty captured us. We found out about it on the last day of our journey, and I was determined to see it before we left the country.

Our guides at the hotel had told us that this beautiful place was five hours away, through the winding mountain roads and over several dangerous bridges. So, we awoke at dawn and began our journey. After driving trucks for a living, I was confident I could navigate the difficult roads and terrain in plenty of time to get there. According to my calculations, we would arrive at the waterfall half-way through the afternoon at the latest.

I drove us through the winding mountain roads like a madman, but all my crazy driving was for nothing as we arrived at our first sign of trouble: the first 'bridge' was no bridge at all, but a car ferry across a wide lake. *And the next ferry did not leave for another hour and a half.*

We took some pictures by the beautiful ferry, and I tried to enjoy the view and the journey. Truthfully though, I was not enjoying any of it, because my sole focus was achieving my goal (getting to the waterfall) and I wouldn't be satisfied until we (I) made it there.

Determined to make up our lost time, we were the first people off the ferry. We stopped at the toll booth on the mountain road, where the operator informed us: despite my calculations that the waterfall was an hour away, it was more like *two hours* with the muddy roads.

As we drove, Kimiko asked me, 'Do you want to go do something else? I just want to spend time with you, it doesn't matter what we do.' I shrugged her off as if she'd just suggested we ride a wooden horse, instead of experience something truly spectacular.

We (I) were going to make it to the cascading waterfall.

I began to snap at Kimiko, irritated at even the slightest inconvenience. I wish I could say I was enjoying the journey, but I wasn't. Instead, I was angrily focused on how quickly I could make each turn in the road, instead of enjoying the beautiful vistas around us. I could not get my mind off of my goal, and with the sun passing overhead, I knew we did not have much time.

We finally arrived at the trailhead to the waterfall, but as we got out of the car, we saw that even the man and woman running a roadside stand nearby were beginning to pack up for the day.

I asked them frantically, 'How do I get to the waterfall?'

'It's too late.'

'How do I get to the waterfall?!'

'It's too late. Come back tomorrow.'

'We leave in the morning, and now is the only time! HOW DO I GET TO THE WATERFALL?!'

'The waterfall is several miles away. It is about to downpour, and the trail is not easy. It is a very bad idea. You can't make it there and back. There isn't enough light, it is very dangerous. You will be in the middle of the forest with no one around to help you if you get in trouble.'

But I refused to listen to them. Instead, I pulled Kimiko with me, ignoring the ominous clouds that gathered overhead, and the rapidly-fading daylight.

I had now traveled for over eight hours to experience this beautiful cascading waterfall, and it was too late to turn back or admit defeat.

Even Kimiko's patience began to wear thin as we trekked through the mountains. I am sure she asked if we could just stop and go somewhere else multiple times along the muddy trail, but she might as well have asked a statue, because I just kept going.

As we crossed the first bridge, it started to rain. I stopped to get a photo of her running across the bridge, and then I ran on. It was muddy and hard to get good footing after the bridge, but we kept going. Occasionally, I looked back to see if I could still see her.

We passed two other travelers, on their way back down the mountain. I asked, 'Is it worth it?' and they replied, 'It's amazing! But you will never make it in time.' I told Kimiko to walk back with them, and I pressed on.

I took off running. It started to rain, but I ran harder. I came across a pond in the middle of the path, and I could barely get around it. The light was getting worse. I kept running hard, although the hills were making my legs burn. I got to the top of another one, and reality finally set in.

I *could* make it to the cascading waterfall, but then I would have no light for a difficult (even with sunlight) trek back.

I was in the middle of a foreign country.
There were wild animals in this forest.
Kimiko was worried sick, and I had abandoned her.
It was pouring rain.
I had not eaten all day.
The rainstorm was killing the last of the sunlight.

I was not going to reach my goal.
I would not experience the cascading waterfall.

I screamed at the top of my lungs. I cursed the rain and Croatia. *I sacrificed so much to achieve my goal, and I was so close, but I knew I needed*

86

to turn back. I screamed and cursed it all again and... I finally turned around.

John, this is where I learned the truth about partially controllable goals: they are very alluring, but very dangerous. Things like winning, rebounding, sales, or beating your opponent's records, can distract us from what is more important: the person we become on the journey.

That day, my focus was on the partially controllable goal, and I spoiled the journey, my character, my health, and my relationship in the process. I compromised the things that are not only important to me, but the things I spend my life trying to teach others to do well.

Cascading waterfalls in life are sexy and alluring, and I hope you get to experience some of them. But if we focus on them instead of true mental toughness, we so often end up compromising all the things that truly matter. Sometimes we make it to the waterfalls, many times we do not. But regardless of whether we achieve our goal or not, there is always a path of destruction in our wake.

TRUE MENTAL TOUGHNESS:

-HAVING A GREAT ATTITUDE
-GIVING YOUR VERY VERY BEST
-TREATING PEOPLE REALLY REALLY WELL
-HAVING UNCONDITIONAL GRATITUDE
-REGARDLESS OF YOUR CIRCUMSTANCES

It might be easier to justify that wake of destruction when you achieve the goal, but it is even more of a reality check when you do not. John, a wise man once said, 'You can go chase a dream, but then sometimes you look back and there's a trail of tears behind you. And the tears are usually your wife and kids.'[12]

I have no wife and children, but that day I learned the truth: that focusing on partially controllable goals can be much more trouble than it is worth!"

John nodded, looking up as the night sky faded down around them. The light was now gone for shooting, but he felt relieved and his body felt lighter.

"Thank you, Akira-sensei. I think I needed to hear that. I can really get derailed sometimes when I get so focused on what I want."

Akira nodded, "I know, John. I still have to re-learn this lesson too sometimes."

John grinned, "So maybe one day we'll *both* learn?"

Akira just smiled back, "Yes, John. Let us hope so."

---

12 – The wise man is Mark Richt (Head Coach of Georgia Football)

27

The Fight!

One day during lunch, the apprentices gathered in the dining hall as usual. But in the midst of some good-natured joking, Katsuo crossed a line, talking about how John had "choked" in the last tournament. John didn't hear a single word after that. His blood boiled, and before he knew it, he had tackled Katsuo!

They rolled wildly across the floor, food flying, each trying to land a punch. As the other apprentices pulled them apart, John made one last lunge. But Katsuo dodged, sending John slipping past him on the slick floor, then crashing to the ground. As he fell, John heard a hollow *pop!* followed by a wrenching bolt of pain, as he felt his arm shatter into two pieces.

Later that day, after the doctors had finished setting his arm and had sent him back from the hospital, John was sitting in his room when Akira arrived. John looked away, unable to meet his sensei's eyes. He felt ashamed, he wasn't ready for a lecture.

But instead of a lecture, the old man seemed to be filled with joy. "John, it's great to see you! I know you wish the circumstance were different, and believe me, I know how you feel. I was a hot head growing up as well, and I got in plenty of trouble. It took me a long time to learn how to live by *principles*, instead of *feelings*.

Many years ago, I even found myself in a place just like the one you are in right now. I had been knocked out, my face was split open, and my nose was broken, by a man much larger than myself. But I chose to believe it was in my best interest and an opportunity to learn and grow. That mindset helped propel me towards becoming the man I am today."

"Wait a second!" said John, "You can't just say something like that and skip over it!"

Akira just smiled, "That is a story for another day. Right now we have more important things to think about. Did you know that the Chinese symbol for danger and opportunity are the same?"

John shook his head, as Akira continued, "At every crossroads there are at least two choices: to view your circumstance as a calamity, or to view it as an incredible opportunity. The most important question to think about right now is this: five years from today, will you be ashamed of how you shrank from what you saw as a calamity? Or, will you look back and be proud of how you maximized your incredible opportunity?"

John nodded, but couldn't stop the tears that began to sting his eyes. "I can't believe I was this stupid! Why did I have to break my arm? I'm trying to believe this is in my best interest and an opportunity to learn and grow, but it seems impossible to believe right now!"

His sensei pulled up a chair beside his bed. "I figured you would feel that way, so I thought maybe we could talk about chasing lions on snowy days."

John couldn't help chuckling. "I don't know how that's going to help, but let's hear it."

Akira continued, "The thing about incredible opportunities is that they often come to us disguised as five-hundred-pound lions. Right now you are face to face with one of the many lions you will encounter in life. The question is, what will you *believe* about it, and what will you *do* about it? There is an ancient story about a warrior named Benaiah, and while he doesn't get very many lines in the Book, they tell us a lot about life. In the first line, it says that one day he chased a lion into a pit on a snowy day, and killed it. The next line says that Benaiah went on to become King David's chief bodyguard.

When most people come face to face with their opportunities (lions) they run as fast as they can in the opposite direction, but when you decide to embrace the lion and chase it, you have the opportunity to build your resume, your character, and your skills.

John, no one is interested in watching a story where the hero doesn't have to overcome a lot of adversity. That would be incredibly boring. We were born to chase the lions and climb the mountains in our life.

Do I condone you getting into a fight? Not at all! But we all have different challenges in life, and now you have found yourself here. I would never *want* someone to come face to face with a lion on a snowy day, but I can tell you one thing: if I were the king, I would want the guy who had the courage to chase and kill the lion to be my bodyguard.

Right now, you have an opportunity to develop mental, emotional, and relational skills in a way that you never would have had you not suffered this physical setback. But what you do with that opportunity, is up to you. Will you squander it wasting time, or will you harness the opportunity and allow it to build you into more of the person you want to become?"

John grinned, sounding more like his old self, "I want to harness the opportunity!"

Akira nodded, "Good." He walked to a cabinet, and pulled out a pen and notepad. "I want you to make a 'can do' list of all the things you can do to get better while you are not able to train. I would start with reading at least fifteen books off this reading challenge.[13]"

John nodded, then started thinking about all the things he could do to get better while he was injured. He started writing...

- *Visualization exercises*
- *Listen to guided imagery*
- *Do highlight film study of my best shots*
- *Film study of other great samurai archers*
- *Encourage my teammates*
- *Write articles about the lessons I've learned during my time training and the lessons I'm learning through the injury*
- *Strength training areas not affected by my injury*
- *Hand-eye coordination exercises with my other arm*
- *Study Wisdom*

As he finished, Akira looked over the list, then nodded in approval. "Those are a few great examples, and I am certain you can think of many more over the next couple of days. Now, I have to get back to the range, but it sounds like you have a 'can do' list to start getting to work on."

"I sure do," John said. "And thank you for helping me see this as an opportunity. I'll do my best to take it on... just like a lion on a snowy day."

---

13 t2bc.com/challenge to download the T2BC Reading Challenge

28

Principles instead of Feelings

A few days later, John returned from his check-in at the hospital with his arm in a cast and a recommendation from the doctors of four weeks of no strenuous physical activity, followed by eight weeks of only light physical activity.

As he grabbed his lunch in the dining hall, Akira came up alongside him with a to-go carton. "How about we go for a walk?"

John was happy to comply, as they took their lunch to a massive tree on the property. Under its shade, they ate in silence for a while. Then Akira asked, "John, do you remember me talking to you a few days ago about how it took me a long time to learn to live by principles, not feelings?"

John nodded, quietly acknowledging that he had.

Akira went on, "Like I said, just like you I had quite a hot head when I was younger. I made many stupid and careless choices that caused others and myself much pain. Thankfully, I had a mentor in my life who brought me out of that, and taught me about living by principles. When I was about your age, he had seen me react to several different situations.

Finally, he asked me a very simple question: 'How is your strategy of living by your feelings working out for you?' I got very quiet, and had to admit that it wasn't working out very well at all. He then shared a quote from a man named Eric Thomas, 'At the end of your feelings is nothing. But at the end of every principle is a promise.'

Living by feelings is never going to work out well for anyone, because feelings change. Sometimes we simply wake up and we feel differently. Sometimes, someone does something to make us feel differently. Living by our feelings is like riding an emotional rollercoaster. When you make the choice to live by a certain set of principles, it will not only protect you from your feelings, it will allow you to step into your greatest potential.

Many days, you aren't going to *feel* like
working out and honing your craft.
Many days, you aren't going to *feel* like treating people really well.
Many days, you aren't going to *feel* like
being unconditionally grateful.
Many days, you aren't going to *feel* like giving your very best.

But the *principle* says you are going to reap what you sow.
The *principle* says that diligent workers are going
to serve kings instead of ordinary men.
The *principle* says to turn the other cheek.
The *principle* says to seek wise counsel.
The *principle* says to speak life and not death.

At the end of principles there is life, freedom, hope, joy, and peace.

The most you can expect from feelings is happiness. But like every other feeling, happiness doesn't last. That's exactly why trillion-dollar industries try to keep you chasing it: because it is perpetually unavailable. If you want to stay on the "happiness train," you must keep coming back to make more purchases, trying to get another hit of that feeling — a new pair of sneakers, a new car, a new iPhone. It is a never-satisfied pit of desire, and if you spend your whole life chasing that fleeting, temporary feeling of happiness, you will miss out on what you really want: *fulfillment.*

Where happiness is easy and "me"-focused, fulfillment is hard and others-focused.

Where happiness comes from a life lived in endless pursuit of feelings, fulfillment comes from a life lived in faithful commitment to principles.

It is healthy to acknowledge our feelings, but when it comes to action, we are much better served to act on our principles rather than feelings.

John, what I want you to do is to seek out principles from ancient wisdom that have been tried and tested through the ages. When you switch from living by your feelings to living by principles, you will start to see very different fruit in your life. It is not easy, and sometimes you will slip up and make choices based off of your feelings. Pick yourself up, and get back on the road to living by your principles rather than your feelings. It's not easy, but —" he nodded to John's cast, "—it is a lot better than living by your feelings!"

John laughed in agreement, as Akira went on. "Now, can you think of four principles you have learned so far from your time here that you want to live by?"

John started to think deeply. He finally replied, "One: you are building your own house. Two: to play present, you must train to live present. Three: you must surrender the outcome and commit to the process or you will become your own worst enemy. And four: no matter what my circumstances are, always chop wood and carry water."

Akira smiled, "My ninja! Those are excellent! I am happy to see our time together is paying off. Now, each day when you wake up, before you enter the shooting range, or before you compete, write out four to six principles that you want to stick to no matter what. Stick them in your pocket, and if you feel yourself wanting to live by your feelings, either touch that pocket, or pull them out and say them aloud of few times by yourself. Got it?"

"Yes, Akira-sensei," said John. He was excited to use this new tool.

29

Warrior Dial

A few months and many reps of the can-do list later, John was finally cleared to train fully again. The night before, he was so excited he could barely sleep.

The next morning, Akira joined him as they walked to the range together. "I am so excited for you to be back out here shooting, John, and I'm sure you are too."

"You've got that right!" John nodded, bouncing on his feet as he walked.

Akira smiled. "Just remember, excitement is very powerful. It can help you, or hurt you. It all depends on how you use it."

"What do you mean, Akira?"

"Well, there are two concepts I think it's important for me to share with you that I'm not sure you're even aware of.

The first is 'labeling.' How you label your internal feelings makes a massive difference in how you filter their meaning. If you get butterflies in your stomach and your hands start to sweat, you could label that as you being 'nervous' and 'unprepared,' or you could label it you being 'excited' and 'prepared.' But rest assured, how you label it is going to directly impact the meaning you give those feelings. A wise man once told me, 'The words we use to label our experiences are a filter to meaning.' The most important thing is rarely what we experience or feel, but rather the meaning we give that experience or feeling. We can give them beneficial and constructive labels and meaning, or we can give them destructive and unhelpful labels and meaning. Which one we give, is up to us. We rarely have full control over the things that happen to us in life, but we do have the power to determine what those events and feelings mean to us."

"I'd never thought of that before," John nodded, understanding. "What's the second concept?"

"It's called the warrior dial. Think about your warrior dial as being from one to ten. 1 is ultra stealth mode, and barely moving. 10 is a super-hyped kamikaze screaming and running into a building with a bomb strapped to them.

Every one of us can turn our warrior dial up or down, and depending on the context of the situation and where we are at our best, we would be wise to do so. Think about today. Based off the context of the day and it being your first day back, where do you think you are at on the warrior dial?"

John thought for a second, then answered, "I am probably at an eight or a nine."

Akira nodded his head in agreement. "And where do you think you need to be to be at your best, and not get re-injured?"

John replied, "Honestly, I'm not sure. Growing up I had always been taught that you were supposed to get hyped before games by watching movies like *Braveheart* and listening to upbeat music. I've never really thought about this before."

"Then I am glad we're talking about it now," said Akira. "I think the best samurai archers would tell you that your best shooting will happen around a four or a five. If your dial is too high, you are more likely to miss your targets."

John nodded, trying to process what he had heard, while simultaneously wondering why he had never learned this growing up playing sports. "So, how do you turn your warrior dial down?"

His sensei smiled wide, "I was hoping you would ask. You can turn your warrior dial down by doing deep-breathing exercises, talking slower, lowering your voice, listening to classical music, and slowing your movements. In fact, many of your teams in the west would benefit from turning their dial down before the "BIG" games and turning it up before the "smaller" games. You already know how to turn your warrior dial up by watching inspirational movies, listening to upbeat music, and by jumping around. But in my experience, it is more challenging to turn your dial down, than it is to turn it up. It will take practice, but you will get the hang of it."

John grinned, "Thank you, sensei! I'm excited to try it out today."

Sure enough, as soon as John gripped his bow, a surge of energy flowed through him. Remembering Akira's lesson, he breathed deeply, and hummed a slow song, calming his mind and letting the oxygen in his lungs quiet his nerves. That simple exercise was enough to steady his hand as he nocked an arrow, drew, and released, sending the arrow slamming into the bullseye!

It felt good that all of his mental training was paying off, but it felt even better just to get back out on the blocks and be able to chop wood and carry water again. It seemed as if John was finally learning to fall in love with the process of becoming great.

30

"They"

As the years passed, John kept training with focus and perseverance. In cold weather and warm, he kept chopping wood and carrying water. In wind and rain and sun and storms he kept beating on his craft, focusing on mental training when the weather was too rough to shoot, and shooting four hours each day, every day. And before he knew it, John had nearly spent ten years at the samurai community. He was very close now to graduation.

One day at dusk, just as the sun was setting, John was finishing up his shooting when Akira approached, watching his apprentice with great pride. As John finished his shooting, he and Akira walked back to the dining hall.

As they did, Akira said, "John, you are very close to finishing your training now. You will graduate as a samurai archer soon, and then you will dive back into the world. Before you do, there is something I must share with you."

"And what is that, Akira-sensei?" asked John.

"I want you know that when you get back into the world, you will face a unique challenge. You will face the challenge of 'they.'"

John just blinked, curious. "Who are 'they'?"

"John, we come out of the womb creating and exploring. But then we start school, and we are told to sit down, shut up, and get in line. We are told to behave and to color inside the lines. We are told to dream sensibly and to be 'realistic.'

You want to know who 'they' are? *'They' are the ones saying all of that.* And if you don't obey, if you don't do what 'they' say, they call you disobedient, unassimilated, disturbed, or they diagnose you with ADHD. Then they drug you, all to get you to fit in their nice little box.

'They' called a coach named John Wooden crazy when he tried to run a press for the entire game. 'They' also thought it was crazy he didn't scout opponents; rather, he chose to focus on letting the other team worry about stopping his team.

The board at Apple ran Steve Jobs out of the company calling him crazy and reckless. Twelve years later, months away from bankruptcy, they came crawling back begging him to come back and save them. He took Apple from the fringes of bankruptcy to one of the most successful and innovative companies of all time.

'They' wanted to have the man committed who came up with the idea of television. 'They' thought the idea of a 24-hour sports network was stupid and could never work. 'They' called Nelson Mandela a terrorist, and 'they' called Jackie Robinson much worse. Rest assured, 'they' will call you all sorts of names, they will throw down the gauntlet in front of you, they will do everything they can to keep you inside their 'safe' container.

If you put one crab in a bucket, it will crawl out. If you put multiple crabs in a bucket, they will pull each other down every time one starts to crawl out. If a crab continues to try and crawl out of the bucket the other crabs will break its leg.

Unfortunately, John, we live in a society of crabs.

But we weren't created to sit still and learn the 'right' answer. We were created to explore, create, to love and to learn.

Be courageous, and never listen to 'they.' Once you break out they will call you a genius, and tell everyone how talented you are. They will try and neatly sweep all your years of sweat, turmoil, and uncommon persistence under the rug. Why? *Because it is so much more comfortable to believe talent is reserved for the chosen few than it is to work your ever-loving butt off to become the best you are capable of being."*

And most importantly, please don't try and teach your friends and family the lessons you learned here."

"But that doesn't make any sense?" Said John.

"John, you must understand the importance of context. There will be people who ask you for wisdom, but you must never cross boundaries without an invitation. A wise man once said "the difference between a pest and a guest is an invitation."[14] You have gained so much wisdom while you are here, but most people won't be interested in learning or changing.

It is very sad, but you need to be prepared for what you are walking into. If I were the best heart surgeon in the world, and my best friend had a heart problem that only I could fix, does that give me permission to do surgery on him?"

John was puzzled, but eventually said, "I guess not."

"Exactly! I would still need *permission* to perform heart surgery. Even though you are equipped with life changing wisdom that could transform

---

14 Dr. James Richards quote

lives, you must not share it without an invitation. Most people just want to be heard and loved, they don't want your wisdom, and that is OK! Sometimes, you can actually become the greatest impediment to other people growing when you try and force things on them. In time, if they see you model it, they will probably start to ask. I have never seen this ancient wisdom fail to come true, *when the student is ready, the teacher appears.*

But I'll share something with you I have never shared with you before. I don't ask your permission to share wisdom with you, because of the nature and context of our relationship. However, with my friends and family, I always ask "would you like my opinion or do you just need to be heard and want me to listen?" Sometimes this annoys them, and just because I could help, I must make sure they need it, want it, and give their permission.

Trust me John, disregard this advice at your own peril. We get letters from former apprentices all the time, and this is the biggest challenge they face when they reassimilate back into the 'real' world." Said Akira.

"Thank YOU Akira-sensei! I will do my best to always be a guest and never a pest!"

3 1

Climbing Mountains

One night after John had finished his chores at the shooting range, he was walking back to the dining hall when Akira found him, waving him down.

"John! Could you come over here please? I have a gift for you."

John walked over to him, curious. As he approached, Akira handed him a small gift box, wrapped in rice paper and string.

"I've been meaning to give this to you for a while now. It's something very valuable that I very much want you to have before you leave this place."

Excited, John untied the string, and, smiling wide, opened the box. Suddenly his smile wavered as saw what was inside: a simple grey stone, totally unremarkable.

"It's... a stone?"

"Yes. But not just any stone. That stone is from the top of Mount Fuji, the first mountain I ever climbed. I want you to have it, as a reminder to always climb the mountains in your own life. Climbing mountains is difficult, costly, and dangerous. And if offered the choice between difficult, costly and dangerous, or safe, cheap, and comfortable, most people will choose the second option. But if you want to become great, you must consistently be willing to do what others will not.

Meraki (may-rah-kee) is a Greek word that means doing something with passion and soul. How many people do you see engaged in *meraki* at work, school, or in sports? The majority of people are disengaged and just going through the motions. They have given away their power and believe their development and opportunities are up to everyone else. That is a lie.

You are more powerful than you realize, but you are going to have to go against the grain, and a lot of people are going to be angry and want you to just sit down, shut up, and do what you are told.

But if you want to be great, you must be willing to boldly step away from the crowd and take personal responsibility for your own journey and development. Like this..."

Akira leaned down to the ground, and used a stick to sketch the following picture:

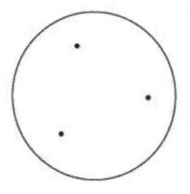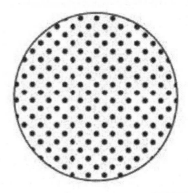

"Look at these two circles. Imagine that the dots in each of these circles represent people.

How replaceable are any of the people in the circle on the left?

Virtually impossible, right?

Now, how about the circle on the right? How replaceable are each of those people?

Highly replaceable, right?

If you're learning and doing what tens of thousands of other people are learning and doing, then *even if* you are the very best, you're still highly replaceable. When you go on a self-directed journey, you're learning things and developing skills that make you highly *irreplaceable*. Even if you aren't the best, it's still very hard to replace you.

Mediocrity is replaceable. Greatness is not.

Most people will never do what greatness requires. Most people will never climb their mountains. But John, we only get one lifetime. And maybe I'm crazy, but I believe the pain of regret lasts much longer then the pain of temporary failure or setbacks. I'm not promised tomorrow, and I want my life to reflect that in the way I live today. I wish more people lived that way. I wish more people would just stop pretending that they get to live twice!

John, the point of life is not to arrive safely at death. Don't believe that lie. On your deathbed you will regret the mountains you chose not to climb. You won't regret the bumps, bruises, broken bones, and scars you got from the ones you did climb.

Of course, there will always be valid, legitimate and responsible excuses not to climb the mountains. But you must choose to climb them anyway. Mountains were meant to be climbed.

Sure, it will inevitably take longer and require more effort than you ever realized at the outset, but it will also be infinitely more worthwhile, not because of what you will achieve, *but because of who you will become through the process.*

When given the option to stay comfortable where you are, or risk the cold, injury, and more, most people choose comfortable. But I hope that instead, you choose to do what others won't, and eventually you will be able to do what others can't.

I hope that at every opportunity you get, you choose to climb the mountain and chase the lions in your life."

32

The Map is not the Territory

During his last weeks in the community, John tried his best to soak everything in, knowing that he would be leaving soon.

One sunny afternoon, he and Akira went for a hike along one of their favorite routes, up into the surrounding hills. They had done this hike many times, but took it extra slow this time, wanting to soak up every second. As they rested at the top of the hill, John looked out over the view, shaking his head in amazement.

"It's so different from when I first arrived. Those trees weren't even as high as my shoulders —" he pointed to a soaring cluster of maples, "— and the big oak that blocked our view for the first few years is gone now. We can see a whole new ridge!"

Akira nodded, "Indeed. Much has changed, and you've only been here for ten years. Imagine how I feel!"

They laughed, as Akira continued: "It reminds me of a truth you'll soon find useful as you move on from here. You will enter a world where society (education system, media, marketing departments, big businesses, parents, friends) will do its best to give you a 'map' by which to live your life. This map points out how things are done, what the rules are, and where the boundaries exist. But the problem is, the world has changed and continues to change more in year than it did in a generation not so long ago. The map is not the territory any more. It's an outdated and some what useless map."

"Really? How so?"

Akira paused for a second, lost in thought. Then he looked into John's eyes, intently.

"Let me tell you a parable. A long time ago, all the farms in the world were owned by a few very powerful people. Only the elites or the knighted (talented) ones were able to rent the land and the tools and were allowed to reap the profits, while the rest of the world worked the land for generations, believing that they didn't have the talent, the money, or the relationships to farm on their own. Thus, they believed they were entirely dependent on the elites who owned the farms.

So all day they worked fields they didn't own, and every night the elites gave them addictive things to numb the pain from squashing their passion and not pursuing what set their souls on fire. The elites shamed anyone who stepped out and tried to do something on their own, ruthlessly maintaining their system that insured the status quo.

But over time, everything started to change...

The tools that used to cost tens of thousands of dollars began to improve, until they were available for free or pennies on the dollar. The land that once rented out for millions of dollars, eventually became available for free or pennies on the dollar.

When a small band of brave workers figured this out, they ran to tell all their friends who had jobs at farms, or were standing in line to get them. They thought everyone would be grateful to hear the good news, but instead, no one believed them. They told them they were crazy, and chased them away with pitchforks!

Only a few people who were brave enough, desperate enough, or had never been able to fit into a job on the farms, followed them back.

And while these few brave workers still struggled to understand the rejection of their friends, they decided to just put their heads down and do the work anyway. The first couple years on their own were incredibly hard, sometimes so hard that they wondered if they'd made a terrible mistake. Life with their friends back on the farms with the illusion of safety and security started to look like a good idea. Sure, they hated the work and didn't own the farms, but at least there they had some company and a steady paycheck!

But they kept working faithfully, and slowly, they began to make breakthroughs. The breakthroughs became bigger and more frequent, until finally, after five years of working the land on their own, they started to really reap the benefits. They now had more time, resources, and satisfaction from doing the things they loved on their own schedule. They even reaped enough to start multiplying their farms and starting new ones.

After ten long years, they had become so successful and independent that their old friends, still stuck working on farms they didn't own, barely recognized them. They couldn't figure out how these brave workers, who they'd known all their lives and grown up with, could have possibly transformed like this. But when the brave workers told them how they'd simply put in the work, and reminded them that the farmland and tools were sitting right there, available for anyone to use, they couldn't believe it. So instead, they just called these brave farmers 'talented' or 'chosen,' writing off their hard work."

"I don't quite know if I follow the parable, Akira-sensei," said a puzzled John.

"What it means, John, is that the world has dramatically shifted, and the gatekeepers who used to decide who got power and opportunity have lost much of the power they use to wield. Attention and trust are the two most valuable resources in the world, and for a long time only the people who had real estate on Main Street, an ad on one of the few TV channels, or a voice in one of the few newspapers, could control those resources. But today, with tools like websites, blogs, online stores, YouTube, Instagram, and self-publishing, attention and trust can be built by anyone willing to put in the work. Things that used to be virtually impossible to build and create on your own can now be done with just a few clicks.

But still, very few people have woken up to that truth, because doing so requires getting uncomfortable and breaking away from much of what they've known their whole lives. They would rather have the perceived illusion of safety with a consistent job, even if it's one where they are completely disengaged doing things they don't believe in, all while complaining about how unfairly they're being treated, despite being able to quit at any time!

They have been so brainwashed by a system that encourages disengagement, passing tests, and buying stuff you don't need to impress people you don't like, that they can't see the reality: that there are fields all around them, *just waiting to be farmed.*

Today, you don't need to work on someone else's farm: instead, you can farm the whole world doing the things *you* are incredibly passionate about! All it costs is your full engagement, and the sweat equity of doing tremendously hard work for years in a row with very little return on your investment. It requires going out on your own and studying the territory from those who are successfully navigating the new world we live in. It requires persistently and consistently experimenting with the strategies and wisdom you learn from them. Yes, it will take longer than the instant gratification of a 'normal' job that will give you table scraps at best, but eventually the harvest can be yours.

But very few understand this, because they have been studying old maps their whole lives, instead of waking up and exploring the rapidly changing territory on their own."

John was amazed, "Wow, I guess I'd never thought of it like that."

"John, this is why it's so important to understand that *the map is not the territory.*"

Akira gestured to the beautiful vista in front of them, "Just like this view has changed, so has the world. But most people would rather trust their old outdated map than do the hard work of exploring the territory on their own, and finding out what it really is and what is actually possible.

John, one large research study found that 74% of people will knowingly give the wrong answer, just to not stand out and be ostracized by the group. This is why most people wander around cluelessly, stumbling into roadblocks and ending up at the wrong destinations, wondering why no one told them that the territory is entirely different from the maps they memorized.

You have been lied to and told that if you ace the test on the map, you will be prepared for the territory, but who would you rather have as a guide? The person who studied an old map for 25 years, or the person who has studied and survived in the territory for 25 years? The map is easy. Anyone can read a map. Navigating the territory is the hard part!

Now, I've done my best to equip you with a toolbox to help you as you navigate the territory alone and map it for yourself: a compass. An internal one, built on the principles and timeless wisdom of 'chop wood carry water.' You have learned the value of beating on your craft, being bold and courageous, always asking 'who says?' and you have truly fallen in love with the process of becoming great. As you go out into the world, you will need these tools more than ever to find your way."

"I don't know how I could have ever done it without you Akira. I am eternally grateful!" He grabbed his wise old teacher and gave him a bear hug.

33

A New Name

By the time he neared graduation, John had become one of the most accurate archers in his class. He was able to pack the bullseye with a cluster of three arrows, even at a far range. Finally, after ten years of training, John had become a samurai archer!

After his graduation ceremony and before he left the community to travel back home, John and Akira took one last long walk through the grounds. They passed many of their favorite locations, spots that John had come to love during his time there.

As they walked, Akira told him how proud he was, saying, "You know now that excellence is within your reach, John. It is accomplished through deliberate actions, ordinary in themselves, performed consistently and carefully, made into habits, compounded together and added up over time. I learned this from a coach in your country who won twenty-one national championships[15]. He said that greatness is a bunch of small things done well, added up over time, that most people think are too small to matter. As a matter of fact, I have one final story for you to demonstrate the power of being deliberate and consistent with the small things!"

John let out a giant belly laugh, "of course you do!"

---

15 Anson Dorrance

"I can't help it!" Laughed Akira.

"So, in 2004 nine Michigan hospitals decided to experiment with a new procedure, and in just a few months it had reduced the infection rates by 66%. By a year and a half over 1,500 lives and over $75 million dollars had been saved[16]."

"Wow! That is incredible! Was it a new innovative technology or drug?" Asked John.

"Nope. It was a simple checklist of five items. You could say it was their *chop wood carry water*. The item at the top of the list was *wash your hands*."

"No way! We figured out that washing your hands could prevent disease and save lives in the middle of the eighteen hundreds!" John practically yelled at Akira.

"Exactly John! Society will always push us towards what is new and innovative and the next big thing, but immense power and potential is harnessed through focusing on doing the simple and small things with incredible consistency and discipline. Don't fall for the traps and counterfeits. Never forget what you have learned here. Focus on the process. Trust the process."

Tears and emotion started to flood over John, as he barely got out, "I'm going to miss all those stories, and I'm not sure how I'm going to do life without you Akira!"

"John, you have learned to fall in love with the process of becoming great, to take the rough side of the mountain, and to let your skills and character be refined by the day-in, day-out process of chopping wood and carrying

---

16   The New England Journal of Medicine, Vol 355, No 26 (Originally read in James Clear's article, *Do More of What Already Works*)

water. I am so proud of you! You will flourish in the world. You have been trained well."

John couldn't stop smiling, as his sensei's words resonated inside him. This was one of the most satisfying days of his life, not because of what he had achieved, but because of the man he had become in the process.

Akira wrapped him in a big hug, then said, "Before you leave, there is one more thing we must do. I want you to close your eyes, put your hand on your heart, and take some deep breaths. I want you to think about all the names you have gone by in your life. Each of those names probably represents a part of your personality. And I want you to think: which of the names represents the strongest, kindest, and most authentic version of you?"

John obeyed, closing his eyes and taking a deep breath. Finally, he opened them, and said with resolution, "Jonathan does. Growing up, my family always called me Johnny. That's the very playful side of my personality, but also a very immature version of myself. Eventually people started calling me John, but that side of my personality is kind of soft and a pushover. I think that Jonathan is the best version of myself."

Akira smiled, and said, "Then from now on tell people that your name is Jonathan, and do not allow them to call you anything else. Names are very powerful. In the Bible, many people experienced name changes, and those name changes were very pivotal moments in their lives. You have transformed through your time here Jonathan, and you need to have a new name that represents that transformation. I am excited for all the journeys you will go on from here, and I trust that you will impact many people's lives in the process. I am honored to have known you."

Jonathan nodded, his heart filled with so many emotions. He embraced Akira one last time. Eventually, he let go, grabbing his bags to leave.

"Akira-sensei, I'll never forget my time here. Thank you for teaching me how to chop wood, carry water, and to fall in love with the process of becoming great!"

"My blessing *Jonathan*," said Akira with a big smile and a few tears...

YOU are more powerful than you'll ever realize. Act accordingly."

The end....

Warning

Shortly after hitting publish, this story quickly became a viral sensation with hundreds of thousands of people reading it in the first year alone with no marketing or traditional publisher. The danger with this book though is that the short chapters can create the illusion that your journey to mastery will be quick or as easy as the turn of a page. It can even make you feel like everyone will arrive at their desired outcomes.

My fear is that you would leave this story on the high of starting the process, but give up when the reality of the challenge sinks in. This can happen anywhere from day 2, to month 119.

The process is simple, the journey is not. I feel the need to remind you that the simple things that bring about mastery, greatness, and many of the outcomes we want, are often like doctors washing their hands before entering the operating room, easy to do and easy not to do. At many points along the journey, the process loses its sexiness and appeal. It's not sexy to wash one's hands, but it saves lives and millions of dollars by reducing the spread of infection and diseases.

You can't *just* read Chop Wood Carry Water and expect that to be enough. You must take what you read and *apply* it. Please go ahead and read it five, ten, fifty times, and I believe it will hit home in different ways every time, but you must actually *apply* what you learn. You must start to experiment with what chop wood carry water looks like in your life. *You have to do the work.* As Nick Saban says about greatness, "it takes what it takes."

If you want to be among the 1% who actually beat on their craft and start implementing what you learn, we've created the #ChopWood90 Challenge to help you on the journey. You can download the challenge at t2bc.com

Please....

Stop pretending you get to live twice
Stop getting by with average
Stop settling for easy
Stop settling for counterfeits
Stop living someone else's life
Stop chasing other people's versions of success

Start pursuing excellence
Start beating on your craft
Start doing what you were created for
Start becoming relentless in the pursuit of what sets your soul on fire.

Love,

Joshua Michael Medcalf

PS: I look forward to hearing from you about the impact it has had in your life as you *apply* the wisdom from within.

Twitter: @joshuamedcalf
Instagram: @realjoshuamedcalf
Cell: 918-361-8611
Email: Joshua@traintobeclutch.com

If you are interested in leadership, life-skills, mental, or sales training programs based on the *Chop Wood Carry Water* principles, please fill out the contact form at t2bc.com/Joshua

Keynote Speaking- t2bc.com/joshua

Mentorship Program- Our mentorship program isn't a good fit for everyone, but we are always willing to see if it is a good fit for you. It is a serious investment of time and resources. Email Joshua@traintobeclutch.com for more information.

T2BC Reading Challenge- People are consistently transformed by going through our challenge! Available under the *free stuff* tab at t2bc.com

The Experience- *Transformational Leadership Retreats*. We bring together people from all over the country to engage in a day of interactive learning. We also create space for fun activities like golf, surfing, or snowboarding with Joshua and Jamie. Visit t2bc.com/experience for more information and to see when the next retreat will be.

The Clutch Lab- Our T2BC podcast takes a deeper dive into leadership, life-skills, and mental training.

T2BC 101 Online Video Course- With over 20 short video sessions, you can use this course individually or to teach your team the T2BC curriculum. It is a great next step tool. Available at **t2bc.com/training**

Join the T2BC community- This is the best way for us to provide consistent value to your life and for us to develop a long term relationship. You will get articles, mp3's, videos, and other tools as they come out. It's also free. ☺ Join at t2bc.com

Books- You can always order signed copies of any of our books by emailing us, and they are also available on iBooks, Kindle, Amazon, and through our publisher.

The first book we wrote is, ***Burn Your Goals***.
The second book we wrote is, ***Transformational Leadership***.
The third book I wrote in conjunction with this book is, ***Hustle***
The fourth book Jamie wrote is, ***The Principle Circle***
The fifth book I wrote with Seth Mattison is, ***The War at Work***
The sixth book I wrote in the same vein
as this one is, ***Pound The Stone***.

YouTube- Our channel is *train2bclutch*

Thank You's

I'm incredibly grateful to my mother, who has supported me and been one of my best friends my whole life. Thank you for never giving up on me when no one would have blamed you if you had.

Thank you to my father, who did the best he could with what he had.

Thank you Judah Smith for being the most amazing pastor a person could ask for. You have taught me so much about Jesus, and how He really feels about me. I don't think anyone has ever had such a profound impact on my life in such a short period of time as you have.

I'm so grateful to Jamie and Amy, you both have been such an amazing support system in my life, and I'm so grateful I get to spend so much time with you. Thank you for creating a safe space for me to be me devoid of judgment.

Thank you Lisa for always being there to hear my articles, or just to listen to another one of my crazy stories, and for being an incredible best friend!

Thank you Steph for being an amazing woman full of love, empathy, and creativity. Your childlike spirit encourages and inspires me every day. Your sunshine lights up the world ☺

Thank you to Tim & Laura for being a living representation of the love and grace of Jesus!

Thank you Amber for always listening to my stories. It's pretty amazing to hear about how you have grown so much in the last couple of years ☺

Thank you to Austin, TJ, Kyle, Joe, Pooter, Krause, Brady and my many other friends who have been there for me during the many low points in my life.

Thank you Anson for all your words of encouragement, and for allowing me to work with your program.

Thank you Russ and Skip for all the mentorship over the years. Thank you Skip for being one of the first people outside of my family to financially invest in me and my dreams.

Thank you Andy and Terry for teaching me so much as a teenager. I wouldn't be here today without your love and wisdom.

Thank you Jacob Roman for clearing your schedule to transform my horrific grammar and at times incoherent thoughts into something people will love and treasure!

Thank you to all the people who have given me the great privilege and responsibility of mentoring you and speaking into the lives of those you lead. I have learned so much, and I am truly grateful for the opportunity to work with you.

Thank you to Tim McClements for never giving up on me at Vanderbilt, and helping me get a scholarship at Duke. I was a royal pain in your ass, and I'm forever grateful you stuck by my side.

Thank you Adri for all your prayers and friendship.

Thank you Tonja for believing in this story and getting it into tens of thousands of people's hands!

Thank you Jesus for your extravagant, reckless, relentless, and undeserved love

Made in the USA
Lexington, KY
20 June 2017